The Mo

Praise f

It was only a matter of time befo.
is an audience for whom *Exile on Main Street* or *Electric Ladyland* are as
significant and worthy of study as *The Catcher in the Rye* or *Middlemarch*
… The series … is freewheeling and eclectic, ranging from minute
rock-geek analysis to idiosyncratic personal celebration — *The New York
Times Book Review*

Ideal for the rock geek who thinks liner notes
just aren't enough — *Rolling Stone*

One of the coolest publishing imprints on the planet — *Bookslut*

These are for the insane collectors out there who appreciate fantastic
design, well-executed thinking, and things that make your house look
cool. Each volume in this series takes a seminal album and breaks it
down in startling minutiae. We love these.
We are huge nerds — *Vice*

A brilliant series … each one a work of real love — *NME* (UK)

Passionate, obsessive, and smart — *Nylon*

Religious tracts for the rock 'n' roll faithful — *Boldtype*

[A] consistently excellent series — *Uncut* (UK)

We … aren't naive enough to think that we're your only
source for reading about music (but if we had our way …
watch out). For those of you who really like to know everything
there is to know about an album, you'd do well to check
out Bloomsbury's "33 1/3" series of books — *Pitchfork*

**For reviews of individual titles in the series, please visit our blog at
333sound.com**

**and our website at http://www.bloomsbury.com/
musicandsoundstudies**

Follow us on Twitter: @333books

Like us on Facebook: https://www.facebook.com/33.3books

For a complete list of books in this series, see the back of this book

Forthcoming in the series:

and many more …

The Modern Lovers

Sean L. Maloney

Bloomsbury Academic
An Imprint of Bloomsbury Publishing Plc

B L O O M S B U R Y

NEW YORK · LONDON · OXFORD · NEW DELHI · SYDNEY

Bloomsbury Academic

An imprint of Bloomsbury Publishing Inc

1385 Broadway	50 Bedford Square
New York	London
NY 10018	WC1B 3DP
USA	UK

www.bloomsbury.com

Bloomsbury is a registered trade mark of Bloomsbury Publishing Plc

First published 2017

Library of Congress Cataloging-in-Publication Data
Library of Congress Cataloging-in-Publication Data
Names: Maloney, Sean L.
Title: The Modern Lovers / Sean L. Maloney.
Description: New York : Bloomsbury Academic, 2017. | Series: 33 1/3 |
Includes bibliographical references.
Identifiers: LCCN 2016034528 (print) | LCCN 2016035356 (ebook) | ISBN
9781501322181 (pbk. : alk. paper) | ISBN 9781501322198 (ePDF) | ISBN
9781501322204 (ePUB)
Subjects: LCSH: Modern Lovers (Musical group). Modern Lovers.
Classification: LCC ML421.M6 M35 2017 (print) | LCC ML421.M6 (ebook)
| DDC
782.42166092/2--dc23
LC record available at https://lccn.loc.gov/2016034528

ISBN: PB: 978-1-5013-2218-1
ePub: 978-1-5013-2220-4
ePDF: 978-1-5013-2219-8

Series: 33⅓

Cover design: 333sound.com

Typeset by Fakenham Prepress Solutions, Fakenham, Norfolk NR21 8NN
Printed and bound in the United States of America

Track Listing

Side One:

1. "Roadrunner" (4:04)
2. "Astral Plane" (3:00)
3. "Old World" (4:00)
4. "Pablo Picasso" (4:15)

Side Two:

1. "She Cracked" (2:53)
2. "Hospital" (5:31)
3. "Someone I Care About" (3:37)
4. "Girlfriend" (3:51)
5. "Modern World" (3:40)

Contents

Acknowledgments

This book wouldn't have been possible without Mandi Maloney, my exceptionally talented, overwhelmingly beautiful, and unbelievably patient wife. She has been listening to me rattle on about the Modern Lovers for a decade and a half and I couldn't have done this without her love and support. A big thanks to my parents, my sisters, and all of the aunts and uncles that have always encouraged my nerdy pursuits. (Or at least put up with them.) Thanks to my friends Mike Ebner, Linwood Regensburg, Maura Johnston, Eugenia Williamson, Seth Graves, Ashley Spurgeon, Jeff Zentner, and everybody else that indulged my authorial neuroses while putting this together. High fives to every editor that's ever given me work, but especially Tracy Moore, Steve Haruch, Patrick Rodgers, Adam Gold, Chris Faraone, Dan McCarthy, and everyone over at Bloomsbury because they let me write about my favorite band at one time or another. Shouts out to Ann Powers, Eric Weisbard, Ryan H. Walsh, Brendan Toller, and the Boston Public Library for research help. Undying, eternal thanks to the Modern Lovers themselves for making a record that gets more exciting with every listen. And thank you to the city of Boston, which made me into the rock 'n' roll loving weirdo I am today.

Introduction

When Jonathan Richman was shouting what would become the count-off heard around the world, kick-starting the punk era from the driver's seat of his Roadrunner, Boston was a very different town. Hardly the affluent, innovation-obsessed liberal bastion it is known as today, Boston was a city teetering on the brink of collapse, an aging city grappling to define its identity in a rapidly changing world. Likewise, *The Modern Lovers*, the collection of demos that would be hailed as one of punk rock's foundational documents, is an album of urban exploration and the search for self-understanding in the maelstrom of contemporary change.

The Modern Lovers is a bundle of nerves and contra-dictions, a genuinely optimistic outpouring of angst and confusion set to a primal throb of resounding immediacy. The essential conflict is the tug of war between the Old World and the Modern World in the city of Boston, in Richman's soul, and in the minds of attentive Americans. It is a psychic struggle as real today as it was in 1970, which is why, almost forty years since gestation, these songs still thrill. Richman's teenage search for under-standing, both social and creative, would mirror the feelings, hopes, and dreams of music fans across the globe.

Richman would eventually become a different kind of rock star, one that brokered in low-volume honesty and intellect rather than big, loud bravado. He would become a cult hero, crossing paths with the mainstream on rare occasion, his character both beguiling and charming. Though a profoundly gregarious performer, Richman has eschewed much of the modern publicity machine, maintaining a safe distance from the music-industrial complex, cultivating an air of mystery in the era of the overshare. Or, more plainly put, he doesn't do interviews. I can't blame him. The man has been unwaveringly honest in his songwriting for over four decades—the honesty is what makes it special, makes the music personal—and the songs should stand as the record of note. But that's not so easy in a culture where we feel entitled to all the intimacies of our idols' lives.

As a fan and a journalist I've tried to reconcile this situation by using moments where Jonathan has spoken on the record—live recordings, radio appearances, the occasional video interview—as signposts in a state where the roads never lead to the same place twice, where beauty blossoms on the highway late at night. My aim was to relay the myth of the Modern Lovers in context and as truthfully as possible. Richman's is a third narrative, a story that refutes the hyperbole coming from both ends of the spectrum. *The Modern Lovers* is not the story of party-poopin' book-bannin' Boston, or the People's Republic of Cambridge—or the self-mythologizing Southie for that matter—but rather a story about magic and mystery and negotiating what those can mean in the modern era.

Astute readers will probably notice that the chapter headings and the track listings aren't the same. That's because I based my arc off of the 1986 Rhino reissue of *The Modern Lovers*. While the original is a perfect record, I'm a member of the CD generation and the Rhino *Modern Lovers* is my *Modern Lovers*, the album that traveled with me so many times from the suburbs to the city and beyond that it is inexplicably linked with my development as a writer and human. Readers who are even more astute will realize the chapters are in a different order than the songs on the CD. That's because the list comes from the encyclopedic Jonathan Richman fansite JojoChords.com's all-edition listing for *The Modern Lovers*. It was that list that made me *see through the painting* to find the story that became this book. It has been a wild ride through the old world and the modern world and I am so glad you are all going to join me as I turn up the radio and head into the dark Massachusetts night.

Well, alright.
Sean L. Maloney
Medford, Massachusetts, 2016

Roadrunner (Once)

ONE! TWO! THREE! FOUR! FIVE! SIX! In the annals of rock 'n' roll there is no more perfect count-off. Sure The Ramones made the count-off their thing on their self-titled debut but they only counted to four—Jonathan Richman counts to six. Richman didn't just kick rock 'n' roll up a notch when he counted off "Roadrunner," he doubled down, took it to the next level. Not since Sam the Sham had shouted "Uno Dos, One Two, Tres Quatro!" at the onset of Wooly Bully had rock 'n' roll seen such a definitive statement of purpose.

The two notes that follow, an overdriven bam-bam that hits with a force reserved for giant boulders in Wile E. Coyote cartoons, are a clarion call. Inside yourself, deep in that place where your soul and your gut flora are basically a primordial stew, you can feel the bolt of energy. When the chord changes, drops into the rumbling bum-bump-bum-bum-bump-bum-bum-bump-bum-bum-bump and Richman yelps "Roadrunner, Roadrunner," that energy explodes like storm-waves against rocky New England shores. It's powerful and intimidating, violent and beautiful, sudden and startling. And then bam-bam, we shift gears.

Jonathan is speeding along the highway, up 128, up the old state highway that has mutated into a state of the art interstate and back again. You can feel the change in humidity, the bite in the air as the dew point drops and 128 takes us farther on to Cape Ann, beyond the sprawl and the smog that cling to the city of Boston. The road is beautiful, open, a work of minimalist beauty, a contrast from the endless gridlock and ceaseless start-and-stop of streets designed for horse and buggy. The pines blur beyond the edge of the headlights.

The pulse of the music and the pace of the poetics create a zeotropic effect where the listener, however far removed from the reality of Route 128 when it's cold outside, feels themselves within the song. That bum-bump-bum-bum-bump-bum-bum-bump-bum-bum-bump shakes the fourth wall until the listener is sitting shotgun in the family station wagon for a tour of a place where even modern people are haunted by a puritanical demeanor.

And yet our narrator finds beauty, finds joy, finds love on this tour of darkened roads. In a lonely world, our hero finds love on the airwaves, in the music and in the magic of the everyday. It is pure contrarian positivity, a sneering beam of light, an anthem about driving to the grocery store. It is a song about the transcendental nature of pop music and an example of pop as pure transcendence. "Roadrunner" is a prayer for whoever wanted to play rock 'n' roll but didn't see the need for a third chord. "Radio on!" is the mantra for anyone that ever believed in the power of pop music to open up worlds of possibility. The way the drums boom-clack-boom-clack-clack underneath the spartan chords, as the fuzz of the keyboard breaks up in the solo, these are prayers to the gods of rock 'n' roll to deliver us from boredom. And damned if they don't. "Roadrunner" is the clarion call for outsiders everywhere, its Art-Brut elegance a sacred text for rock 'n' roll believers straight from the self-proclaimed hub of the universe, Boston, MA.

Jonathan Richman: I was magnetically drawn there, I had to be there. I'd get there early, watch them rehearse and get sounds, watch them work out songs. But they knew I had to be there—they knew! As obnoxious as I was, it was life and death. They could see in my eyes that it was life and death for this little high school squirt ... I felt that I'd run into people that understand me, as a person that was never understood at all. I wasn't intrigued, it was more like everything changed from that point on.

It is the spring before the Summer of Love and Boston has hit rock bottom. A decade and a half of white flight and urban renewal have decimated the population. The city has lost 10,000 people every year since Eisenhower took office. Industries like shipping and manufacturing, industries that had been the city's lifeblood since colonial times, are disappearing. Entire swaths of the population have been abducted and ejected through eminent domain, sent scurrying as bulldozers level neighborhoods to make way for progress. Families, searching for a safe place to raise children beyond the smog and traffic and chaos of the city, are pouring into the suburbs. The tax base has vanished and city services are disintegrating.

The city is on the edge of collapse.

But the city had not been completely abandoned. Amidst the crumbling vestiges of the industrial revolution and the entropic state of the historic seaport, there are still some folks in love with the city. Some will never leave, entrenched from the moment their people got off the boat, whether it be the *Mayflower* or one of thousands of less esteemed vessels that had brought the Irish, the Italians, the Greeks, and the Russians. Boston is a city resistant to change, a city that clings to the way things were, slow to embrace the new, skeptical of outsiders. It is a city that loves to complain—about the Church, about the weather, about the bums on the baseball diamond at Fenway Park. But these folks, as loud and stubborn as they could be, were of dwindling number and surrounded by the ruins and tarnished trophies of former glories.

The empty spaces that the Old Guard has created through negligence and forced displacement are being filled by a new breed. Artists, grifters, and runaways are flocking to city, taking advantage of absentee landlords, nearly abandoned homes, and slum-rate rents. Musicians, painters, and writers are living alongside college kids and ex-cons, immigrants and soon to be ex-pats, all living on the cheap—making new art, making new culture, making the city elders squirm.

The city had been a principle location in the Folk Revival, Club 47 in Harvard Square was the stage that launched Joan Baez and played host to early unbilled Bob Dylan shows. It was one of the earliest participants in the psychedelic experiments that are shaping the new culture. The city has always been a magnet for the country's best and brightest, weirdest and wildest. Marijuana is plentiful, birth control is readily available, and LSD is still legal—for a few more months, at least. These are heady days. These newcomers may not have been the vice-loving sailors cavorting and fighting in Old Scollay Square but they are sinners and slum dwellers just the same. These are exactly the same people the Old Guard had tried to evict in the first place.

There were weapons to be yielded on both sides. The Old Guard had the Federal Housing Act of 1949, which had been used by the Brahmin's to evict an entire neighborhood of political opponents in the 50s. The full weight of the Housing Act's eminent domain powers and the might of the Eisenhower interstate system are being thrown about to gut neighborhoods. The Old Guard have the Boston Redevelopment Authority. The Old Guard have the Boston Ward & Watch Society and the City Censor. The Old Guard have the courts and the cops, occupancy limits and enough ego to assume moral authority. Their opponents would be armed with art, and love, and idealism of youth.

Jonathan Richman: I grew up in the suburbs of Boston and went wherever I could in Boston when I was sixteen. Just wandered around looking for ways to get into the music scene,[1] And I didn't really know how but I did. I somehow magically did ... when I was sixteen I heard the Velvet Underground and everything changed.

SUMMER 1967: *Chelsea Girls* has been running for almost three weeks when the Symphony Cinema on Huntington Avenue is busted for obscenity. Just up the road from the Museum of Fine Arts in Boston, Symphony Cinema is across from Symphony Hall, catty-cornered by both the mid-construction Christian Science Center with its modernist reflection pool and the South End, a hard-luck Victorian-era neighborhood that was becoming the center of Boston's avant-garde. A shabby

---

[1] Jonathan Richman, *Wax! Crackle! Pop!* Radiovalencia.fm, March 3, 2014.

little storefront theater, Symphony's programming is—depending on whom you ask—either provocatively cutting-edge or peddling smut.

Symphony Cinema is no stranger to controversy either. Months before Andy Warhol's experimental film earns the Pop art provocateur his "Banned in Boston" bonafides, Symphony saw another manager arrested on obscenity charges, this time for screening the softcore Swedish art film *I Am Curious Yellow*. In the meantime, however, the United States Supreme Court had overturned the statewide ban on John Cleland's *Fanny Hill*, or *Memoir of a Woman of Pleasure*. Also the city's battle with William S. Burroughs hadn't gone the government's way and the city censor had been unable to make his last four arrests stick.

A once-impeccable record of persecution and censorship was falling apart quicker than the tower on Fort Hill. Precedent is no longer in the censors' favor but that was no reason to stop the arrests—the publicity is enough to supplant actual accomplishments. The bluster is enough. Bluster has a lot of pull with the constituents. If the City Censor's office had been smart, they would have picked up Andy Warhol when he was in town the week before. Those sorts of headlines would have been great for all involved.

Warhol had been at a venue called The Boston Tea Party, a Unitarian church turned psychedelic ballroom on the other side of the South End, toward the Combat Zone, the city's red light district. (The Tea Party had been up and running for almost five months, making it one of the oldest and most esteemed of the city's psychedelic shacks.) Warhol had been shooting film footage of The Velvet Underground, the New York rock band that had been part of Warhol's Exploding Plastic Inevitable shows. The partnership produced an album on Verve records—a throbbing, droning, distorted piece of avant-garde rock named *The Velvet Underground & Nico*. The band and its music have been hovering around the fringes of the popular consciousness since spring gave way to summer. Some folks get it, some folks don't.

One place that the partnership has proven to be an astounding success is in Boston. Following the Exploding Plastic Inevitable appearance at the Institute of Contemporary Art (ICA) on Boylston Street, a couple of blocks north of the Symphony Cinema, The Velvet Underground would have the attention and ears of astute fans, disc jockeys, and the city's budding music press. When The Velvet Underground returned for their weekend of gigs in May of '67 there were fans waiting for them—a rare occurrence outside of their core audience at Warhol's Factory. The Tea Party, whose management had seen the box office receipts that followed Andy Warhol and associates' appearances at both the old Moondial coffeehouse and the ICA, were booking more Velvet Underground shows before the engagement even began.

Alan Lorber, a producer and labelmate of the Velvets, is creeping around the fringes of The Tea Party scene too, ingratiating himself and scouting talent. His new album *The Lotus Palace*, an instrumental jazz exploration of the new lysergic sounds, is gaining traction, and MGM has offered him his own production deal, scouting talent and cashing in on the youth market. The rumor is that he plans to mirror the regional identity of the blossoming San Francisco scene. The rumor is he's got record deals to give out and albums to make. Boston seemed like a logical place to look for a magical Fountain of Youth Culture, for Lorber, for his bosses at Metro-Goldwyn-Mayer's recording division, and for a young kid from Natick named Jonathan Richman.

Natick is not *in* Boston. Boston-proper is relatively small area-wise, confined as it is by oceans, and rivers, and long established boundaries. Natick is just west of Route 128, on the other side of the unofficial line between the outer-rim of greater Boston and the way-out-there rim of Greater Boston. It is a small town experiencing the upswing of the post-war suburban boom. Swathes of tract houses are springing up where the forests once were, as mortgages and lawns replace renting and triple-decker, three-family housing. An entire generation of city dwellers was tired of the blockbusting tactics of bureaucrats and bankers in the city proper. And Natick is even near Shoppers World, brand new shopping mall.

Natick is not the sort of place that has a high tolerance for oddness. The element of surprise is exactly what the parents had hoped to leave behind. Safety. Stability. Synagogue on Saturday and work on Monday. It is a place where art isn't considered sensible, where individuality is always suspect, and straying from the freshly paved path to consumerist nirvana will not be encouraged. Natick is Middle America. Middle America is stultifying.

Natick exists, like any other town on the outer fringes of any other city, in a cultural void. Any culture that does creep into the small towns on the edge of the metropolitan area has been stripped of its fecundity, so separated from its originating actions that it seems to appear out of thin air. You won't find too many abstract expressionists at the soda shop or many minimalist composers creeping around the Woolworth's. Art is a thing that happens elsewhere. To make music that aspires to be more than just muzak for make-out sessions, you've got to get out of town.

For a kid with a creative temperament, for a kid that wants more out of life than punching a clock and grinding out widgets, there isn't much to do in the suburbs but get in the car and drive. When art is the motivating factor in your life, like it was for Jonathan, you can't just sit at home and hope that someone discovers you. You have to take your art, however half-formed, to where other people are creating their art. Your parents may encourage your art, your friends may enjoy your art, and your teachers may tolerate it, but without other artists to exchange ideas and knowledge, your art's potential is rather limited. Whether you make literary, visual, or sonic art, it will wither and die if you don't transport it from the fallow tracts of single story ranch houses and plant it somewhere more fertile.

But suburbia does have its saving grace: radio doesn't stop at the city limit. For Jonathan Richman, a gaunt, gawky teen short on social expediency and long on philosophical questioning, radio would be the street-lights along his path out of suburbia. WRKO, WMEX, and WHDH were baptizing the suburbs in the sounds of the city, in the sounds of faraway exotic places. "Melancholy Music Making Man" by the Righteous Brothers, "Six O'clock" by the Lovin' Spoonful and The

Velvet Underground's "Sunday Morning" all beaming from the transmitters to Jonathan's ear. It is the spring before the Summer of Love and the seeds of punk rock have been planted.

Boston Globe: Cambridge Mayor Daniel J Hayes Jr urged an all-out crackdown on hippies Monday Night. "We must eliminate these people from our city," he told a city Council meeting. He cited an increase in drug arrests and an exodus of longtime residents as two of the chief reasons. The Mayor's speech came in the aftermath of narcotics raids over the weekend, at one of which a 19-year old girl was found in a closet suffering the effects of LSD. But for heat and emotion it did not rival an earlier portion of the meeting during which members of a group sponsoring an anti-Vietnam war resolution on the ballot were labeled as "creeps," and "refugees from a barber shop."[2]

---

[2] Robert J. Anglin, "Hippies, Peace Petition Spark Outrage, Scorn at Cambridge," *The Boston Globe*, October 3, 1967.

Astral Plane

"Astral Plane" is not as explicitly Massachusetts-themed a song as say "Roadrunner" or "Government Center" but it is the one that ensures Richman's place in the pantheon of great New England poets. "Astral Plane" is the moment that connects Jonathan Richman with the legacy of the Transcendentalists, with Thoreau, Dickinson, Alcott. Richman, in a state of constant seeking, re-imagines the boy-doesn't-meet-girl tropes of rock 'n' roll tradition and finds a spiritual solution.

In his lecture "The Transcendentalist," a treatise on the Unitarian splinter group that would go on to shape American cultural and political thought for generations to come, Ralph Waldo Emerson told those gathered at the Boston Masonic Temple in January of 1842: "As thinkers mankind have ever divided into two sects, Materialist and Idealists … the idealist takes his departure from his consciousness, and reckons the world an appearance." Richman's own lyrical departure opens up the possibility of overcoming romantic rejection, of prolonging an unrequited love.

The rhythm undulates beneath "Astral Plane," tension building and releasing before the end of each bar, wobbling between ethereal and corporeal. The drums are focused but wary, as somnambulist blue-notes squeeze through the distortion of the keyboard; the bass bobs like a buoy on a breezy day, the energy of the group becoming "a phantom walking and working among phantoms." The listener too is brought into this phantom.

Where "Roadrunner" is The Modern Lovers' Walden-esque tribute to nature (however paved and neon-bathed it may be circa 1970), "Astral Plane" creates a response to Margaret Fuller's "Sacred Marriage" for the Sexual Revolution. Richman needs to overcome the physical in order to attain the love he yearns for, needs to project beyond the material world and his own shortcomings to be worthy of reciprocal love. "Astral Plane" unlocks a new dimension in one of pop music's enduring themes.

FALL 1967: *Praise Ye The Lord.* It is a strange backdrop for a strange scene, but there it is, etched in marble. The Boston Tea Party wasn't the city's first psychedelic ballroom—that would be the Psychedelic Supermarket, a parking garage repurposed to host the city's first Cream show—but it is the one that matters. There is The Unicorn in the Back Bay, The Crosstown Bus in Brighton by Boston University, but those venues were tangential. The Tea Party is *the* scene, the place with the best light show, the best bands, the best crowds. The Tea Party is a magical space, where light and sound become cosmically entwined, stretching and shifting the fabric of space and time around the audience.

The Tea Party is on Berkeley Street in a formerly swanky section of brownstone bow-front townhomes that's been on the downward swing as the twentieth century wears on. A former Unitarian church, the sandstone facade bears a six-sided star in a window the size of a man. The star serves as a talisman and anchor for the swirling film and oil projections of The Tea Party's acclaimed, immersive light show, a rune of protection in a neighborhood as gritty as any. What the neighborhood lacked in wayward sailors looking for red light thrills it made up for in junkies and debauchery. The Tea Party isn't on the fringe. The Tea Party *is the fringe*.

The Tea Party is where the New York Crowd hang when they came through town. The room had been consecrated with the experimental films of Jonas Mekas, Stan Brakhage, and the Filmmakers' Cinemathique. Warhol and his friends—including a young press agent and Harvard dropout by the name of Danny Fields—are there pretty often. Mel Lyman, Jim Kweskin, and the cadre of young artists and oddballs behind *Avatar*, the art-deco astrology-rag being hawked on every street corner in the city, are all there. Paul Williams, the publisher of mimeographed fan magazine *Crawdaddy*, and the crew of folks that will launch rock-crit broadside *Fusion* are here. This isn't a teen center or a frat party or nightclub in the traditional sense—no schmoozey torch singing here. No one is sitting down, nothing is inhibiting you from interacting with the art as it is being created. This is something new.

In the back, beyond the marble exultation to "Praise Ye The Lord" that frames the whole affair, there is another social experiment going on. All alone sits a man who calls himself Woofa Goofa, spinning records. Whatever records he wants, in whatever order he wants, he plays them. No sales data or magazine charts influence Woofa Goofa's playlist, just his own deep knowledge. Radio has never sounded this anarchic, this authentic. This isn't the

WRKO or WMEX, which even at their most creative and adventurous are still building playlists off of retail sales data and listener requests. The Top 40 art as viewed through the lens of technocracy.

There is a science to the Top 40 that maximizes listenability in order to maximize profits. 'MEX and 'RKO had been battling for teen-market supremacy lobbing 45s of Vanilla Fudge and Sergio Mendes at one another. 'MEX and 'RKO are analyzing data and deciding that the Amboy Duke's "Journey to the Center of the Mind" and José Felicano's cover of The Doors "Light my Fire" are what's happening *right now*. What Woofa Goofa is pedaling is more magic than science. This is something more, something visceral and new. This is WBCN, broadcasting at 104 megahertz on the FM dial. This is the American Revolution.

The iconography of revolution is easily co-opted though, especially by the interests of the status quo. By the time international entertainment corporation MGM ran their first advertisement, the Bosstown Sound was done. It's not that bands like Ultimate Spinach, Orpheus, and The Apple Pie Motherhood Band weren't revolutionary. Given the long lens of history it's clear that the kitchen-sink approach to psychedelia, which strives to insert as many ideas-per-minute as musically possible into every song, would seem like the "it" thing to executives that had cut their teeth in an earlier era and couldn't make heads or tails of where culture was going. Virtuosity and complexity feel important even when they miss the mark in terms of relevance and vitality. Virtuosity and complexity also have a very limited audience when they aren't accompanied by some sense of relatability. For all of the intellectual success of Ultimate Spinach and the other bands that Lorber signed and MGM lumped under the Bosstown Sound banner, their commercial success was always doomed.

It's not that the bands here weren't operating within a revolutionary vernacular in their own over-educated way—they were all making baroque-folk-jazz-rock that was ahead of its time—it's just that the revolution had already been fought and won on the West Coast. Radio support never materialized, partly because the hip corners of the Top 40 were already occupied by West Coast bands like The Doors and Jefferson Airplane. Then there was the ad in the *Wall Street Journal*, painted with all the panache and inherent hipness of an insurance pamphlet: Colonial soldiers in full regalia. Tri-corner hats and bayonets don't hold the same allure for rock 'n' roll fans as love and freakdom. MGM's ad campaign, its entire PR strategy, missed the mark by a million miles— colonialism is not, and never will be, groovy.

Bands from Boston had been getting signed by major labels for years. Barry and the Remains had cut for Epic Records, The Lost had cut for Capitol, but Alan Lorber and MGM had tried to plant their flag and claim the entire city for their own. What they got was a chimera of unassociated groups making unassociated music while pretending to be a naturally evolved organism. Lacking the factory-like focus of L.A. or the radical history of the San Francisco scene, Lorber and MGM's monster flails wildly for a moment before whimpering away.

The city's music scene is cynical. The transition from a folk-based economy has not been smooth. A lot of people have been burned by the industry, a lot of people are just burned out. Psychedelia got here first. Timothy Leary, Ram Dass, the whole Internal Freedom Foundation group had operated out of Harvard before they were run out of town. LSD may have been criminalized and demonized by the media now, but the seeds of the city's music scene in the age of acid were sown years ago.

By the time acid culture hits the mainstream, Boston is all tripped out. Things are starting to get twisted. Rumor has it Mel Lyman—who played harmonica with Kweskin's Jug Band—locks his followers in a room and feeds them acid just to watch them freak out. Times are dark, the city is crumbling around them and the music reflects that, but in a malingering sort of way. Songs like "Ballad of the Hip Death Goddess" by Ultimate Spinach or Earth Opera's "The Red Sox are Winning (Kill the Hippies)" are grizzled, over-intellectualized attempts at indulging and insulting contemporary values. There's a sneer that doesn't fit the complicated song construction and ambitious arrangements.

MGM, ABC, and Elektra are rolling into town trying to graft the sunshine aesthetic of West Coast pop to the cold and gray of New England bitterness. It is a doomed move. This brand of psychedelic maximalism swallows too many sounds—too much folk, too much jazz, too much rock—to squeeze back out in any recognizable shape. The reality is there is no Bosstown Sound, only an advertisement and an awkward attempt on Alan Lorber's part to capture a different coast's zeitgeist, only an advertising department's uncreative attempt at packaging unrelated items.

Selling Boston as a hotbed of hippie bliss was never going to work anyway. By the fall of 1967, the straight establishment in Boston is openly at war with the counter culture. Charles Street is the locus of square ire, one of the city's oldest neighborhoods and a youth culture hotbed. Charles Street and the surrounding Beacon Hill neighborhood were spared imminent destruction in the name of urban renewal earlier in the decade thanks to cunning uses of historic preservation and neighborhood mobilization. Now the neighborhood has other problems. It is the kind of place where young people congregate en masse, the sort of place cops can pick up two-bit drug dealers and college kids alike. Rents were cheaper when the neighborhood was still on the chopping block, still in the crosshairs of a city intent on branding the neighborhood a slum and using its blighted status to demolish the entire area just like they had done to the West End in the 50s. But the battle to preserve the historic neighborhood and its ageing structures had been good for business, the public discourse a positive for the retailers and residents that maintained the neighborhood's vitality over the years. Charles Street has eluded the fate of the West End, its housing and businesses will not be plowed under to make way for luxury apartments.

Now the neighborhood is swarming with unsupervised suburban teens, drifters, grifters, and freaks eating, shopping, and living. Since the spring of '68 more and more people have been camping out on the Common, an outdoor extension of the Charles Street action. A repository for the disenfranchised, the Boston common camp has its own underground economy, nestled somewhere in the Venn Diagram of fashion-forward shopping center and red light district. The Boston camps are swelling with runaways and dropouts. Human flotsam and jetsam is washing ashore on the steps of the state capital building atop Beacon Hill.

On the other side of the river, the Cambridge Common serves a similar function. Just west of Harvard Square, the Common was built as a forum for community. The tradition of public discourse and public performance, that brings the youngest and loudest of rock bands to the Common, has its roots in the earliest days of the colony. The Common was built for democracy—exactly what those tri-corner hats had fought for—a space where citizens voice their opinions to their peers. By the late 60s it had become a hub for up and coming performers.

Jonathan Richman: My dad had a few jobs. He was a travelling salesman. He represented food chains that sell to the military. Which is slightly different ... some of the companies are the same. But the military has its own grocery stores. So he would be a salesman to the military grocery stores. And the military bases would sometimes have their bingo games on Friday nights, so he had a sideline of bingo prizes and things.

And that's how I got a guitar. It was a ten dollar guitar lying around the house, and he said, hey John you want this guitar? It was in the shed and I'd just go: [at this point Jonathan starts strumming the guitar and laughing] *for hours just enjoying the sound. And I was transfixed by it. And I just started making stuff up.*[1]

I started singing in public in Boston in 1968, I knew I couldn't sing or play like the other guys did but I didn't want

---

[1] Arielle Mullen, "Interview with Jonathan Richman," Sythesisweekly. com, August 23, 2015

to. I figured I had feeling and that was enough. I knew I was honest.[2]

In an ocean of longhairs adorned in paisley and fringe, here was a clean cut kid banging out crude, single-chord songs. On the Cambridge Common, awash in a sea of ideas each more malleable than the next, here was this kid with short, close-cropped hair and a white plastic motorcycle jacket. In a space where folk songs like "Tom Dooley" and "House of the Rising Sun" clamored for attention alongside rambling blues jams, this kid with the bright eyes and the big smile was singing about everyday objects in a nasal monotone. One can only imagine that the audacity of this Art Brut approach raised the ire of the many classically trained musicians milling about. It is as freaky and far out as anything in that lysergic scene, a counter to the counter culture, a point of focus in the blur of cultural experimentation.

What Jonathan had discovered, by chance or on purpose, is the secret to rock 'n' roll success: keep showing up. Keep showing up when nobody cares, keep showing up even when your audiences don't react the way you want. Keep showing up, keep making art no matter how far you are from the artistic mainstream. Idiosyncrasy helps but consistency is what turns hobbies into careers. One of the great myths in American entertainment is the myth of discovery, this idea that someone powerful will sweep in and declare "this person is genius" and make you a star. Discovery doesn't just happen

---

[2] "Jonathan Richman, Twin Tone Records bio," accessed July 7, 2016, http://www.twintone.com/richman.html

magically; you have to put yourself in the place where people are paying attention. As Jonathan bangs out his one chord wonderings week after week, people start paying attention.

Mayor Daniel J. Hayes was behind the raids on Kinnard Street, the biggest battle in his self-declared War on Hippies, and an explicit attack on the spirit of experimentation and cultural dynamism that defined Cambridge. The police had gone building to building, arresting, beating their way through house after house of young people. The Diggers, an anarcho-art collective of political radicals and rock 'n' rollers, took the brunt of the attack. The row houses that run along the southern edge of Cambridge's Central Square neighborhood are filled with young people willing to flout occupancy laws—and morality laws—in search of cheap rent, or better yet, a place to squat. Kids looking for a place to live, a place to fit in, a place of their own. As novelist and activist Kay Boyle wrote in her 1975 novel about battling both the government and the Lyman Family *The Underground Woman*, "what were the youth doing but huddling together in fear?"

Most landowners on either side of the Charles River had fled to the suburbs after the war. Most operated as absentee landlords, unable to get financing from the city's lenders, disinterested in maintaining properties of little value. Devalued properties lead to low tax rates and less money to spend on civic improvements. Nobody wants to live there but broke students and freeloader types, et cetera. Long story short: hippies were to blame for depressed property values, not the other way around. As luck would have it, however, calling in the goon squad is not a successful re-election tactic. Not even in the sweaty, screaming realms of local Massachusetts' politics would Hayes' tactics succeed. *Praise Ye The Lord.*

Jonathan Richman: I moved to New York when I was 18 to be near the Velvet Underground and that whole Andy Warhol art scene. I thought I would do art with them but what really happened was I spent the 10 or so months I lived there, more or less alone, walking around after work. [Andy] actually invited me, said come on down when you finish high school and work on movies and things. But by that time things had changed. He had already been shot and wasn't physically participating in the movies.[3]

I wanted to be that—near that whole New York scene. I had already been auditioning at local coffee houses and they weren't interested—maybe because, like, I couldn't play or sing or anything. That might have had something to do with it. So I moved into the cockroach-infested Hotel Albert where rents were cheap and it was rich in musical heritage. The Lovin' Spoonful at one time practiced in their basement, Lothar and the Hand People practiced in their basement—so I practiced in their basement. And I wanted an audience, see, because— some people don't like attention. I'm not one of them. Me and attention, we get along pretty good.[4]

I opened a show for [The Velvet Underground] once, before I had a band. There was an opening act that didn't show up and the promoter—who was a friend of ours from western Massachusetts—I was riding up with them from New

---

[3] Jonathan Richman, *WYEP* interview, October 28, 2015.
[4] "Jonathan Richman," accessed July 7, 2016, http://thehotelalbert. com/rock_roll/jonathan_richman.html

York. The opening act didn't show up so they looked around the room and I was there. [laughs] *They looked at me and I said sure, can I borrow a guitar? And Lou Reed handed me his Gibson Stereo guitar and I did about twenty minutes. And Sterling Morrison said 'Well, Jonathan that was quite remarkable'. 2015.*

WINTER 1968: Tensions between the Old Guard, the entrenched interests, and the New Guard's growing demands for attention are mounting back in Boston. The publishers of *The Avatar* are brought in on obscenity charges. The newspaper is a mix of esoteric astrology, avant-garde culture with anti-authoritarian undercurrents and a flowing Art Noveau influenced design. *The Avatar* set out to be the mystical mouthpiece for Boston's underground scene, part Aquarian recruiting tool and part arts magazine.

Their vendors—the scruffy kids selling *Avatar* on every corner, wandering through traffic trying to make a nickel a paper—are picked up on both sides of the river for peddling smut. The paper responds with a full page that simply says FUCK SHIT PISS CUNT. More vendors get arrested and blustery red-faced blowhards like Judge Adlow of Boston get more explicit in their anti-youth denunciations. City Council representatives are screaming for heads, and cops entered every encounter with billy clubs at the ready.

There are stories of cops being surrounded by gangs of roaming hippies, scraggly longhairs roughing overzealous, undermanned police details on Charles Street. *The Boston Globe* and the *Boston Herald Traveler* devote pages and pages to the hippie problem. Panicked and outnumbered, the establishment, the conservative core of Massachusetts politics that stretches back to belt-buckle hats and pantaloons, rears its ugly head.

There's talk of a city-wide curfew and bringing in the National Guard to clear the squatters on the Boston Common. Alternative encampments are offered up in parks and city plots on the outskirts of town. By the Fourth of July the camp has been gutted, cops in riot gear—jackboots and leather jackets, batons, helmets, the whole costume—barreling their way through the crowds of peaceniks, cracking skulls and making arrests. It is open season on longhairs. It doesn't matter if they are camping out or passing through: hippies are the enemy. Officers on horseback rounded up stragglers and marched them to paddy wagons, the cops beaming with the smug self-assurance of the paid thug.

The attacks on Boston's youth culture aren't just coming from the outside though. The violence is coming from within as well. One night at The Tea Party on a Velvet Underground bill featuring the MC5—the young Detroit revolutionaries being groomed for Elektra records by Warhol associate Danny Fields—a riot broke out. The Up Against the Wall Motherfuckers—a belligerently anarchistic political action gang in black leather jackets—are in town and ready to rip up the crowd, as revenge for a buddy's incarceration. The Motherfuckers may have been political activists but they were no peaceniks. The Motherfuckers were looking for a fight—and they had perfected the art of antagonism—and it didn't matter if MC5 were onstage. People are hurt, the room is trashed, and the tenuous social pact between performer and audience is shattered for an evening.

None of that compares to the destruction wrought by the Establishment itself. While the residents of Boston and Cambridge barely receive financing for residential projects to preserve their neighborhoods and fight blight, their cities can get seemingly endless financing for large-scale projects, as if the entire government was in the demolition lobby's pocket. Through the Federal Housing Act of 1949, the power of eminent domain, and a gleeful willingness on the part of the banks, Boston and Cambridge can borrow immense sums of money for the eradication of slums. And *slums* may as well have been defined as "homes of political enemies" and "homes of ethnic minorities."

They have bulldozed the West End, evicted a few thousand working class families. They have destroyed brick and mortar that had housed generations of Bostonians, only to put up poured-concrete apartment towers for six or so hundred upper class folks. Scollay Square—the bustling, vibrant home of burlesque theaters and cheap thrills for most of the modern era that had been beloved by sailors and bemoaned by bluebloods for generations—was eradicated nearly a decade ago. In its place sits a cold, bureaucratic plaza known as Government Center and its temple to Brutalist architecture, City Hall.

They're ripping apart the Back Bay, demolishing a blocks-wide strip in a straight line from Massachusetts Avenue to the outskirts of the city. It's the Turnpike Extension and it runs from just past Fenway Park all the way out to Natick where it connects to Route 128, itself slated for expansion and connection to the newly designed Southwest Expressway. There's talk of a third harbor tunnel, a dig bigger than any proposed before.

The key to making all this highway construction/ destruction work, the key to solving Boston's traffic problem—as suggested by both business and bureaucratic interests—is the Inner Belt. This superhighway would run from Chelsea on the harbor though to the Central Artery—the elevated highway that bisected the city—through Cambridge, annihilating the population along the riverside. The Inner Belt would continue across the river, connecting to the turnpike extension cutting through Allston Village, Brookline, and West Roxbury where it would connect with the proposed Southwest Expressway. Finally, the Inner Belt would cut through Roxbury and Dorchester to connect with the recently finished Southeast Expressway, making a circle around the city and displacing tens of thousands of families so that suburbanites wouldn't have to sit in traffic.

But it's the kids that are going to destroy the fabric of society.

Old World

The desire to look back in time and think things were better, the instinct that drives one to be skeptical of the new and untested, is very human. Nostalgia is likely to gloss over the unsightly or untimely, likely to overlook the grit and the grime that clings to the underbelly of an era like piss stains in a dive bar toilet. Nostalgia can wander too close to a fear of the modern, and vice versa; the embrace of modernity can be taken too far. This negotiation is at the heart of Modern Lovers' "Old World." The Modern Lovers, ever contrarian, will embrace both.

If we return to "The Transcendentalist," Emerson reminds those assembled at the Grand Lodge of Masons on Tremont Street across from Boston Commons: "The first thing we have to say respecting what are called 'new views' here in New England, at the present time, is that they are not new but the very oldest of thoughts cast into the mold of these new times." Massachusetts has been wrestling with the encroachment of Old World values on New World realities since the buckle-heads set foot on Plymouth rock. Upending traditions is one of Massachusetts' favorite traditions.

Richman sings that he "still loves the parents, still loves the old world," a concept antithetical to the "never trust anyone over 30" ethos of late 60s counter-culture. His embrace of familial love doesn't jive with his "New York girlfriend," his decision to "keep his place in the arcane"—the antithesis of the entropy and Year Zero mentality of youth culture. Richman looks at "the 50s apartment house" in the "1970s sun" and sees that he can live in multiple moments. Again, Richman is able to overcome the lack of reciprocal love, of true interpersonal understanding, by viewing both moments in tandem.

There is lucidity in this duplicity, allowing Richman the insight necessary to detach from nostalgia—from the old world, from the New York girlfriend, the 50s apartment house—and swing his artist gaze at the future. You could view it as survival instinct, carving out an aesthetic space in your time as a means of not being overcome by prior failures and earlier shortcomings. And it's all set to a throbbing rock 'n' roll dervish from an alternate timeline where people still shouted along to "96 Tears" and bands like ? & The Mysterians were bigger than the Beatles.

SUMMER 1968: In Copley Square there is a hole. Between the stately elegance of the Copley Square Sheraton, the Gothic reverence of Trinity Church, and the streamlined modernity of the John Hancock Insurance building there is a hole and it is growing. There is a yawning chasm in the earth where a city block once stood. The Boston Public Library, austere and elegant with its Renaissance revival archways and palatial stairs, watches over the hole from across Dartmouth Street. The sun shines on Boylston Street, as truck after truck hauls away dirt, removing the infill that transformed the Back Bay from a swampy wetland off the Charles River to the most fashionable location in Victorian Boston.

In this hole will go a building. This hole will become the John Hancock Tower and will displace the recently opened Prudential Center—itself a former hole, where the B&A railyard used to be—as the city's architectural focal point. The building will stretch nearly 950 feet in the air and look like nothing Boston has ever seen. Straight lines and stark edges will rise from the flatness of Copley Square to cut the skyline like a razor. Sixty stories of pure, modern architecture from the minds of I. M. Pei & Associates, the firm that had transformed (and was still transforming) Scollay Square from a ragged red light district into the futuristic formalism of Government Center.

Downtown, passed the Old State House and the colonial-era cemetery just past the Common, construction workers are putting the final touches on City Hall, a colossal poured-concrete ziggurat flipped on its cantilevered head in the heart of Government Center. The Hall's first resident is Mayor Kevin White, newly elected and idealistic. The former Secretary of State for Massachusetts, he's in his early forties and ambitious, a career politician careening into office on a wave of turbulence and change.

His strategies don't rely on the clan-like political machines that have owned Boston since time immemorial; his strategies rely on connecting with people. Listening to constituents and placing their concerns ahead of bureaucratic and business interests is White's modus operandi. He began his campaign at house parties, went door to door canvassing the city, and visited every firehouse in the city, shaking hands and talking with citizens before he even took office.

Jonathan Richman, young Natick native with close-cropped hair and odd musical inclinations, is across the Atlantic, soaking in the sights and sounds of the Old World as it wrestles with the modern age. Shockwaves were still being felt from the student uprisings of '68, the fires of revolt stoked by the radical cut-paste do-it-yourself art movement The Situationist International. The tensions between capitalist, communist, and fascist are as unmissable as the gleaming new buildings erected in the shell of world war ruins. The Old World has a depth to its culture, strata of artforms that you didn't find off the highway in suburban America. It is the kind of place where ideas are born, ideas like starting a band, making that band your job, and committing everything to making your art.

New York City hadn't panned out for Richman. He'd spent more time as a foot messenger for *Esquire Magazine* than at the Factory making art. For a while, he stayed with Steve Sesnick, who'd taken over the role of managing The Velvet Underground after Andy Warhol was fired by the band. Richman had been through Max's Kansas City, where the art-rock oligarchy of Warhol Superstars and underground weirdos congregated in the back room. He'd wandered the streets of Manhattan alone, wandered away from the scene and all the social weirdness it entailed. And then he left for Europe.

Things are changing at the Factory and things are changing with The Velvet Underground. Warhol is out, his managerial brand no longer adorning the band's every move. Nico is out, her droll delivery and Teutonic beauty had never been part of the initial plan. But most importantly, John Cale is out. Cale is the figure responsible for propelling the band beyond the rock horizon, instilling the endeavor with the avant-garde spirit that defines the group's earliest work. His droning viola and insistent, unremitting bass playing gave the band its pulse, its primal throb. His progressive instincts and classical training had taken Lou Reed's Dylan-esque pop ambitions into new and undiscovered realms. Reed may have been the focal point but Cale was the lifeblood, the noise maven that accelerated the group's evolution. And now he was out.

Reed wastes no time in recruiting a replacement. He doesn't have to look beyond The Boston Tea Party scene that had so readily embraced the band to find Doug Yule. Yule is the bass player for The Grass Menagerie alongside former member of The Lost Willie Alexander. He is a friend of Steve Sesnick, the Velvet's tour manager who has slid into Warhol's role in the wake of the pop-artist's dismissal. Yule has a feel for music that perfectly fits into Reed's new plans, and he is rushed into the studio to record the band's third LP, *The Velvet Underground*. The band has been traded up from Verve Records to their parent company MGM, home of the sputtering Bosstown Sound. Reed is writing kinder, gentler material and looking for a hit. The grand experiment of the Cale years is over.

Elsewhere, other exercises in social evolution are coming to a messy and meandering close. In Detroit, the MC5's revolutionary ascendency is crushed with one bellowing "motherfucker!" America, it seems, wasn't quite ready for a rock band leading off a record with the king of curse words. *Kick Out the Jams*, a blistering debut for Elektra Records, was dead on arrival, a publicity stunt gone wrong. Even a master publicist like Danny Fields couldn't turn the tide back in the 5s' favor. John Sinclair—he of *dope, guns and fucking in the streets* fame, manager of the band and leader of the pseudo-revolutionary White Panther Party—is arrested for possession of two joints, complicating the MC5's already tenuous business arrangement. The only interactions the band and their incarcerated manager have are through a young lawyer named Joseph Oteri.

Oteri is a familiar face. Known as "Boston's Pot Lawyer," Oteri has been battling for the legalization of marijuana in the Massachusetts court system for years. It's a battle that has had more downs than ups. Legal weed is a proposal that received an immense pushback but has gotten Oteri in all the papers. Oteri was at the top of the defense list when *Avatar*, that underground newspaper run by folkie-grifter Mel Lyman and his astrology-glazed followers, ran afoul of the law. The city censors had been getting punched up in the court, but that wasn't stopping them from flexing their muscle on the streets. Warhol's *Chelsea Girls*, William S. Burroughs' *Naked Lunch*, and the Swedish film *I am Curious Yellow* had all beat their obscenity raps. *Avatar* would beat its obscenity rap too, especially with Oteri on board.

Avatar, however, is not safe from itself. The publication, part of the newly emergent underground press, is always on the brink, pulled between hip-culture prognosticating and Aquarian mysticism, held in check by a balance of secular outsiders and Lyman's Fort Hill group. Lyman operates out of a decimated Victorian neighborhood deep in Roxbury, twelve houses on a hill surrounding a crumbling Revolutionary War era tower.

From there he dictates his edicts, spouts his Scientologist inspired philosophy and coordinates his own public relations and recruitment campaigns. When the last of the outsiders abandons *Avatar*, Mel takes it as a sign, declares himself a god. Prior to that, his claim to fame was playing harp on the Jim Kweskin Jug Bands' college-folk cover of Chuck Berry's "Memphis." Now he is a deity. Although not one that can keep his underground newspaper in business.

High profile court cases and delusional leadership aren't enough to keep *Avatar* afloat. The youth newspaper market is crowded, the competition stiff. *The Cambridge Phoenix* has a two-year head start and the added heft of being included as an insert to the *Tech* and the *Crimson* (MIT's and Harvard's student papers). *Boston After Dark* works with the student papers on the other side of the river and has the benefit of *Phoenix*'s experience going into its arts-writing-and-ads model. *The Mole*, the far-left rag run out of Cambridge's *Central Square*, is covering hard-hitting, left leaning political news mixed with the underground press' love for conspiracy theories. Dailies like *The Boston Globe* and the *Herald-Evening Transcript* had the square world sewn up. *Rolling Stone* and its Boston-born counterparts *Crawdaddy!* and *Fusion* had the rock scene covered. There wasn't a lot of room for an imparsable paper, however beautiful or divine it might be.

Elsewhere in the city, the power of the people and the power of the political establishment have come to loggerheads. The Inner Belt is not the juggernaut its designers thought it to be. Consternation abounds in state offices as Federal highway money is held up and coffers run dry. Local protests and political positioning have slowed the Interstate beast to a crawl. The proposed highway loop, the one slated to destroy urban neighborhood after urban neighborhood for the ease and accessibility of suburbanites who've chosen to work but not live in the city, looks to be a worse proposition with each reappraisal. From West Roxbury to East Somerville, neighbors were coming together, trying to escape the fate of East Cambridge, leveled for a NASA contract that never came through, gutted for an Inner Belt perpetually stalled.

The voice of resistance was heard all the way up at the State House, high atop Beacon Hill and in the poured-concrete canyons of Government Center. Governor Francis Sargent is a local boy, an MIT grad, and a Republican. He had been Lieutenant Governor for three years before his predecessor was appointed to the Nixon cabinet. Put in the hot seat by Boston mayor Kevin White, whose neighborhood-first strategies have resonated with those in the path of the Inner Belt, Sargent is quick to appease populist demands. There is, after all, a governor's race ready to ramp up and Sargent's most likely opponent is one Mayor Kevin White.

SUMMER 1969: The Boston Tea Party is packing up and moving across town, taking up on the edge of no-man's land between Fenway Park and the newly finished turnpike extension at 15 Lansdowne Street. Ray Riepen, owner of both WBCN and The Tea Party, has taken over cavernous Kenmore Square club The Ark. After a couple of years and a couple dozen Velvet Underground shows beneath the Praise Ye The Lord

engraving, it is time to move out of the old Magna
building, that mystical Unitarian church on Berkeley
Street. At a capacity of 500 (700 if nobody intended to
move) the room was too small to turn a profit without
raising the ticket price or booking lesser talent. In the
two years since the building had transformed from
the Moondial coffee house, the room had developed a
reputation as one of the best on the East Coast, selling
out shows and bringing the world's most cutting edge
artists to the city. People have come to expect a constant
influx of outstanding talent. The rock scene in Boston
is exploding. The Boston rock scene is outgrowing The
Boston Tea Party.

Market capitalism being what it is, rooms across the
city had started booking rock acts. Symphony Hall,
that bastion of proper Bostonian culture, is playing
host to the heavy flute vibe of Jethro Tull, who are on
the cusp of their *Aqualung* world takeover. The Music
Hall has switched from sweet-jazz to the Grateful Dead
and Janis Joplin—two acts that should have been at
The Tea Party. The mayor's office is hosting concerts
of all stripes, from the big rock shows at the Hatch
Shell along the Charles River to gazebos in the deepest
parts of working class suburb Hyde Park, as part of his
Summerthing initiative aimed at creating community
through artistic endeavors.

And then there was The Ark, a massive 1,400-person
capacity room behind Fenway Park's left field wall,
dubbed the Green Monster. It had had an opulent
opening champagne party and scores of investors. It was
the toast of the town's now-crowd for a few months. But,
The Ark is big and couldn't bring in the marquee talent

to keep a club that size going. Riepen and his young general manager Don Law aren't moving the Tea Party in; they're taking over. By the time Jonathan Richman returns from the old world, Boston will be a whole new scene.

Pablo Picasso

The implication that Pablo Picasso "was never called an asshole" is patently absurd. That the notorious womanizer and jet-setting celebrity who upended the world of modern art with radical visions of what could be done with paint and canvas was never called an asshole strains credulity. But when appending the assertion that "Pablo Picasso was never called an asshole" with the sneer "not like you," as Jonathan Richman does, the absurdity is jettisoned and seriousness sets in.

Jonathan turns his gaze directly at the listener, takes a lyrical vision previously fixated on nature, on the spirit, on the past, and turns it directly at his audience. The emotional value becomes greater than the representational value, the listener—so often the protagonist of pop songs—becomes the antagonist. Richman sends a shot across the bow, tells the listener "be not bell bottom bummer or asshole," warns us to "be not schmuck, be not obnoxious," as if he knows the malfeasance in our hearts, the dark deeds that haunt our souls.

The band hangs back like a Greek Chorus, guitars arguing back and forth with the piano, the rhythm section standing at the ready to encourage or diffuse the situation depending on how it might break. As Richman explains Picasso's unwavering magnetism, that he could parade down a sidewalk "and girls *could not resist his stare," the possibility dawns on us that Richman is not in fact admonishing his listener, but admonishing himself.*

Again Richman creates a narrative with multiple viewpoints, a rock 'n' roll reply to the titular artist's early experiments with Cubism. Richman and Picasso very literally share a gaze, both possessing eyes that look through the painting, as it were. Richman collapses art history and personal history into one moment, external observation and self-reflection are folded into one another, awe, and loathing bleed across borders. "Pablo Picasso" ruminates on a single, repetitive riff, dispenses with normative concepts of pop structure, challenges the audience to reevaluate what they've heard and how they listen. "Pablo Picasso," like its titular hero, succeeds in upending the art form in which it was created.

Iggy Pop: I like nothing better than a little joke, and that's what it is. They sit out there telling each other "man those dudes up on stage, they do not turn me on at all." And I can feel that hostility and I feed on that energy, it's really something to work with the hostility of an audience.[1]

FALL 1969: The Boston Tea Party has never seen anything like The Stooges. Hailing from Ann Arbor Michigan, the MC5's baby-brother-band had barely been together for a year. They'd made a record and had a buzz about them but they certainly had none of the polish and chops, the skill and shine, that were paramount to taking the stage at the city's premier psychedelic ballroom. Even

---

[1] Robert Somma, "Four Stooges at the Tea Party: Rock Alienation," *Fusion*, October 17, 1969.

in the early days, when The Tea Party was still sharing space with the yoga scene's headquarters and playing host to wild and wooly locals like The Lost and The Hallucinations, The Tea Party had never played host to such a force. Even the combined powers of the MC5 and The Velvet Underground—a booking that provoked a small scale riot in December of '68—couldn't top the minimalist malignancy of The Stooges.

The Stooges are the newest band on Elektra, scored for the paltry sum of $5,000 in a deal with Trans-Love Energies, the management and promotion company set up around the MC5 by manager John Sinclair. The same Sinclair who is in jail now, facing down ten years for two joints. As a veteran of Detroit's boho set and avowed revolutionary—the White Panther Party—Sinclair had been followed for years, a focus of police attention as the local and national media freaked out. Sinclair has retained Joseph Oteri, the "Boston Pot Lawyer" currently defending *The Avatar* from obscenity charges. The MC5 were taking on the square world and the square world was taking back. But The Stooges weren't caught up in all the revolutionary hype. They were in it for the kicks, the simple degenerate thrills. Their lead singer, Iggy Pop, thrashes about wildly, throwing himself across the room like a mortar lobbed into enemy territory. And they were, of course, a Danny Fields band.

Fields first made his way into the Cambridge scene as a teenage Harvard student: young and smart. He'd dropped out of school, moved to New York, and fell in with the Factory crowd. He introduced Edie Sedgwick to Andy, essentially bequeathing the world its most modern muse. He is the one who'd dug up John Lennon's "bigger than Jesus" quote while editing teen magazine *Datebook*. He is the reason half the country had set their Beatles records on fire. He was The Doors' publicist early on, when they were making *The Soft Parade* and getting kicked off the Ed Sullivan show. Danny Fields was part of the circle at Max's Kansas City, which included Lillian Roxon, author of 1969's massive *Rock Encyclopedia*, and Lou Reed, of course. He has an uncanny eye for cute boys making wild sounds. These days Danny Fields is signing bands for Elektra Records and shepherding The Stooges into the national spotlight.

Jonathan Richman: We would be talking and I would say "You know what I want to be? I want to be a rock 'n' roll star." And [Danny Fields] would say "Jonathan, don't say that." And I'd say "why not, it's the truth?" He says "because people will laugh at you." I go "yeah, and? It's the truth." He says "just don't say that." Why not? We would talk like that. He was trying to be nice, trying to help me out.[2]

David Robinson: I saw Jonathan, like everybody else, in Cambridge Common, at the Sunday afternoon free concerts, in 1970. Jonathan wore a white plastic Harley Davidson motorcycle jacket. That was his trademark. People would say, did you see that crazy guy with the white plastic jacket? They'd introduce him as young Johnny Richman and he'd come out and everybody would laugh, boo, and mostly ignore him. He was terrible, but he was aggressive and wild compared to what else was going on then. A few weeks later he walked into the record store where I was working with a little 3"x5"

[2] *Danny Says*, 2016.

card advertising a band. He decided right then that I'd be the drummer. Jonathan didn't have a standard voice. He just wanted to show the world that anyone could do it. All you had to have was feeling. People thought it took courage to perform alone when you couldn't sing and only knew two chords on the guitar, but it didn't take courage. It was something Jonathan wanted to do so bad, no one could have stopped him.[3]

Ernie Brooks: Anyway, Jerry Harrison and I saw Jonathan a couple times on the Cambridge Commons, but we didn't meet him—and then he showed up at our apartment at 152 Putnam Ave wearing his white plastic motorcycle jacket. Danny Fields, the great facilitator of all things rock 'n' roll, brought Jonathan over, and that was the first time Jerry and I really met him …

So Jonathan was into poetry—but he was also into the first Stooges album, which had just come out. So I talked with Jonathan about what a great rhythm section the Stooges had, and he was really into that, and he was really funny. He also loved the Velvet Underground, but he was very conflicted about them, because of the darkness they presented.[4]

SPRING 1970: Jonathan's *dérive*, his drift from New York to the Old World, is over, his sojourn complete. He is back in New England, making music with a drummer from the other end of Route 128 and the guitarist next door. Drummer David Robinson had gone to Woburn

[3] Scott Cohen, "Funny How Love Is," *Spin*, June 1986.
[4] "Jonathan Richman: In Love with the Modern World," accessed July 7, 2016, http://www.vice.com/read/jonathan-richman-in-love-with-the-modern-world

High School, on the north side of the city's sprawling suburbs. Guitarist John Felice has known Jonathan since they were kids, growing up in the same stretch of single-story ranches and single-family sameness out near Shoppers World, the first open air shopping mall east of the Mississippi River. Rolfe Anderson is rounding out the low end. They've begun augmenting Jonathan's solo performances, adding layers of insistence to chordal binaries and modernist obsessions, providing a primal throb to frame Jonathan's pop-art lyrical approach. The sound picks up where *White Light/White Heat*, the VU's album with the magnum noise-rock opus "Sister Ray," left off—picks up right where the John Cale and Lou Reed had relationship splintered away.

Unsurprisingly, this didn't always go over well with every audience. Rock 'n' roll is in flux, radio is calcifying, freeform is becoming less free and more album oriented. The psychedelic ballrooms require a big crowd, label support, and radio attention to fill up their typical three or four night concert runs. The coffee houses were low-volume folkies. The teen clubs wanted teeny-bopper music, the kind you might hear on WRKO or WMEX. The frats and the college scenes were looking for cover bands that could tackle the hits of the day or some sort of white blues jam successfully sanitized for middle-brow consumption. Rock bands looking to perform bold, new music beyond the fold of popular taste aren't exactly swimming in places to play. Rooms like the Music Hall and the newly baptized, bigger, badder Boston Tea Party are hedging their bets with proven winners. For all of the success that The Velvet Underground had incurred at The Tea Party, little was spilling over onto their avid student and his trio of suburbanites. Felice and Anderson will not last long as Modern Lovers.

The addition of Brooks and Harrison, on bass and guitar/keyboards respectively, solidifies the outfits' intensity, cements their place alongside The Stooges and Velvet Underground as purveyors of the most piercing shards of rock 'n' roll fervor. Robinson's drumming is snappy and straightforward, free of the fills and extraneous cymbals that were taking over FM radio. Boom-clap-boom-boom-clap. Raw chords from Richman's hand-painted Fender Jazzmaster explode from the amplifier. Harrison's piercing leads on guitar and his over-driven electric piano would recall John Cale's fiercest and most dissonant moments on *White Light/White Heat*, weaving through Brook's low-end lurch like electricity searching for the path of least resistance before exploding skyward.

Across town, near Kenmore Square, the new turnpike extension and the new location of The Boston Tea Party, another band is forming. Made up of a group of New Hampshire teenagers led by Steven Tyler and fueled by Rolling Stones fandom, this young band practices day in and day out in their Commonwealth Avenue apartment. They've chosen the name Aerosmith and begun playing the same small town college-and-teen-club circuit as the Modern Lovers. Elsewhere in Boston, Atlantic Records has signed the J. Geils Band—an amalgamation of locals including former Hallucinations' frontman and WBCN overnight DJ Peter "Woofa Goofa" Wolf—known for manic, explosive shows that rival The Stooges in sheer ferocity. Geils' self-titled debut becomes an underground sensation. Meanwhile, Ultimate Spinach, the original standard bearers of the Bosstown Sound, release their final record to little notice.

In New York, The Velvet Underground begin a summer residency at Max's Kansas City. Their debut album for Atlantic, *Loaded*, is in the can but something is amiss. After weeks of playing in their own backyard, on the verge of their newest release, Lou Reed doesn't show up. His tenure with the band is over. Manager Steve Sesnick (former Tea Party manager and friend of Jonathan Richman) has convinced Reed to go solo, to take his songs and shoot for the pop charts. This leaves Sterling Morrison and Mo Tucker—who had missed much of the *Loaded* sessions due to maternity leave—as the only founding members. Doug Yule, John Cale's replacement, would helm the new band rolling out its new record. The Velvets had seen declining returns ever since parting ways with Andy Warhol. No matter what bold new ground they were breaking musically, the band was just not going to crossover in a world where eleven-minute blooze jams and soft rock singles had become the norm.

Meanwhile, the city censors are all hot and bothered again. Back at the Symphony Cinema, where Warhol's *Chelsea Girls* had been slapped with an obscenity rap, they are caught in the controversy surrounding the latest in Swedish cinema, *I Am Curious Yellow*. It's a slow-moving art film, no more salacious than what one might see in the Combat Zone on a Saturday night, no steamier than the burlesque shows that had run in Old Scollay Square before it was bulldozed. The film had been imported by Grove Press, the same company that had fought and won when the Boston censors got their knickers in a twist over William S. Burroughs' *Naked Lunch*, the same company that had similar censorship cases around the country. The sexual revolution hadn't made its way to the stuffier sections of city bureaucracy quite yet.

Mayor Kevin White—the youthful mayor that was baptized by fire in the War on Hippies, the idealistic mayor that (with the help of James Brown) prevented race riots in the wake of Martin Luther King's assassination, the progressive that had built a block-by-block, neighborhood by neighborhood coalition to help break the corrupt, regressive city political machine—is battling the council over an "adults only" ordinance. He has vetoed the proposal that would force all bookstores and newsstands selling "adults only" material to register with the city, a proposal of dubious legality and questionable intent, written with the intention of scaring businesses away from adult entertainment. The council has overridden that veto but that is not the end of the fight.

White has imbued considerable goodwill across the city in the short time since taking office in 1968. Within the first week he was masterfully negotiating an eight-day deep freeze that, combined with the city's dilapidated housing stock, plunged much of the city's poor and working class into treacherous physical conditions. That he was able find warmth and sustenance for so many immediately made him a man of the people. But Mayor White is also caught between the entrenched and intimidating interests of those in the city who wish to pave a seven-mile swath of the city and those who would prefer to remain in their homes.

The battle over the Inner Belt has begun to spill out of individual neighborhoods. Resistant residents from Jamaica Plain to Charlestown have begun to connect, begun to organize. In the spring of '69, a heterogeneous group of Italian, Jewish, Black, and Irish citizens that belied the city's political monoculture shut down the highway that leads to the airport. In Roxbury, at the far end of the proposed route, beneath the ominous Fort Hill tower where Mel Lyman and his cult of LSD-astrologers watched over the city, the destruction has already begun.

Bulldozers are leveling entire city blocks, rooting out families that had been there for generations despite bullying by the Boston Redevelopment Association or the unrepentant prejudice of banks and mortgage lenders. Cranes and dump trucks are carting out the carcasses of once-grand Victorian homes, picking up the pieces of demolished businesses. Roxbury Crossing looks like a war zone and there's still seven miles of destruction set to go.

It would be a shame to waste an enormous amount of Mayor White's political capital fighting a porn-obsessed proposal that will certainly be thrown out of court. White has bigger fish to fry. The Boston Redevelopment Authority has secured grants for the restoration of Quincy Market, the colonial-era marketplace next door to City Hall, and White has plans to turn the decrepit old eyesore into the jewel in Boston's tourism crown. But, more importantly, there's an election in 1970 and Kevin White, young, well-liked, and well-connected, has his eyes on the Governor's Mansion. White wants to be a rock star politician.

Jerry Harrison: There was a certain simplicity in means. It's hard to remember what it was like back then but the music had taken on a rather rococo flavor, a little like it has again with people falling onto the music specialist categories, like studio musicians who do certain things extremely well but often don't have that much to say.[5]

Jonathan Richman: Now one more thing though, we don't want to be forward and ask you to dance with us, unless you want to and that's fine. But there are some groups that actively discourage it partly by their stage demeanor if not coming out and saying "we hate it when people dance." We understand how people could get intimidated over the past four years and hesitate to dance when the Modern Lovers play, thinking it will infringe on our sensibilities. And they think we're not intellectual but we don't mind. If anyone loves to dance you'll love this song.[6]

Steven Tyler: And look at Boston's rock history, starting with J. Geils. It's always been dark, but it always had something mysterious to offer ... I mean, I fucking sat in 1969 in a coffeehouse in Cambridge and watched this guy [Jonathan Richman], *and I remember looking at Joe Perry and saying, "This guy's out of his fucking mind, what the hell is he doing?" Because he'd go on for 20 minutes singing "And the radio's on ..."*[7]

[5] Tim Goodyer, "Looking Ahead," *Music Technology Magazine*, December 1986.

[6] "The Modern Lovers—'Live at Stonehenge Club'—Ipswich, MA, 1970/1971," accessed July 7, 2016, https://www.youtube.com/watch?v=Cd0ZK9Gvy6g

[7] Matt Ashare, "Talking Heads: On the Line with Bosstone Dickey Barret and Aerosmith's Steven Tyler," *The Boston Phoenix*, December 18–25, 1997.

I'm Straight

Countering the counterculture, rebelling against the rebellion, and splintering off of the splinter groups can be a formula for isolation. Easy to praise in hindsight, making the declaration that you're "not like Hippie Johnny" and taking a strong anti-drug stance in the early 70s was a pretty huge fuck you to a lot of rock 'n' roll fans. When the first string of rock stars began dropping like overindulgent, overdosed flies—Hendrix, Morrison, Joplin, not to mention casualties farther down the fame ladder—the Modern Lovers screaming "I'm Straight" was immediately alienating.

While square society are content with the booze and their diet pills and hip society are fine filling up on reefer, acid, and coke, Jonathan Richman pleads to his love interest to consider a third path. Unsure as he is—he has "called this number three times already," he's prepared to feel awkward—Richman is compelled to tell the object of his affection his feelings. Richman makes his case, argues that he'd make a better lover than her current beau.

He's always stoned, Jonathan says into the handset, he's never straight, trying to convey the clarity of his vision over telephone wires. The way Richman's voice tightens up around the word straight, the way he squeezes each reluctant word out as if he regrets every syllable. We don't know who Hippie

Johnny is exactly but we all know someone like Hippie Johnny, the lover that is both magnetic and repellent in the proper light, the classic American bad boy that has never had to plead with a lover.

But Hippie Johnny could, quite possibly, be a stand in for all of American youth culture at that very moment. Temperance had fallen out of favor in secular society in the wake of Prohibition's disastrous unwinding. It would be over a decade until youth culture would create its own hardline sobriety movement. But at the dawn of the 70s, Richman was practically alone in his stand against mind altering substances.

From the bubblegum pop of AM like The Lemon Pipers' "Green Tambourine" to the deep cuts of the progressive rock stations, drugs were everywhere. As a person that loved "modern girls and modern rock 'n' roll," as he explained in "Roadrunner," this cultural preoccupation with getting wasted must have felt like a trap, a pit of quicksand that only Richman could see us sinking into. "I'm Straight," is not just love song but a warning to us all that there is a better way.

SPRING 1971: The hole in Copley Square is beginning to swallow the entire neighborhood. The city-block sized hole in the ground, home to the future John Hancock Tower, is slowly filling itself in, swallowing the earth around it—the ground reaching for an equilibrium that is bringing the entire neighborhood down with it. In the two years since construction, the neighborhood had begun to sink and now the whole place—from the century-old sandstone structure of the Trinity Church to the New England Power & Gas building to the stately Boston Public Library—is teetering on the brink.

This is not entirely a surprise. Copley Square and the surrounding area, collectively known as the Back Bay, used to be a swamp. The Back Bay, home to grandiose brownstones and the stunning new Prudential Center skyscraper where the B&A railyard once stood, was not a naturally occurring plot of real estate. Filled in during the 1800s with dirt, gravel, and detritus from westward railroad expansion, The Back Bay was built over swamps and marsh, ancient Native American hunting grounds, estuaries, and fishing weirs—it was very literally a bay that had been filled in with parks designed by Fredrick Law Olmstead and fancy houses. Fancy houses built on sand, so to speak.

Now, every hole dug for every beam of the almost-framed John Hancock Tower is pulling a little bit of the neighborhood back into it. Lawyers are cracking their knuckles and licking their chops as damages accrue. New England Telephone, Boston Edison, Boston Gas & Electric have all joined the City of Boston in looking for a financial settlement from the insurance company building this paean to corporate ego. Trinity Church has been adding metal braces and new mortar along the tower-facing walls of its facade. The walls of the foundation are being lined with steel plates, measures are being taken to ensure that the water table maintains its equilibrium. And yet work continues: the metal lattices of this future monolith keep reaching toward the sky.

Two blocks north toward the Charles River and three blocks west toward Massachusetts Avenue more earth-shattering changes are occurring at WBCN. The progressive FM station founded in the late nights and early years of The Boston Tea Party, WBCN is now the number two FM station in the market, held at bay from the number one spot by an easy listening station up the dial: WJIB. And while the smooth sounds of Enoch Light may be first in the overall ratings, 'BCN is at the top with the massive youth market. 'BCN has become a national leader in free form programming, a model for those looking to monetize the cultural shift from AM pop singles to album-oriented programming. 'BCN has squeezed blood from rock, has made the underground scene an overground concern. Boston has regained its status as an important music city and 'BCN is leading the charge, picking up where The Tea Party left, carrying that venue's influence and connection over to the airwaves after the ballroom's demise.

Success, of course, never comes unfettered, and the loose and groovy world of underground music is not immune from the discord inherent to capitalism. The Tea Party, headquarters for the city's nascent rock scene, had succumbed to the economics of international touring at the end of 1970. The cost of maintaining a 1,500 capacity and the ever-increasing fees of rock's biggest names was just too much to maintain. The Tea Party had been the first to bring acts like Led Zeppelin and the Grateful Dead. The Tea Party was the beachhead that established rock's dominance on these shores. But that reputation wasn't enough to keep owner Ray Riepen and his investors in the black. Word on the street was that Riepen is $100,000 in the hole after The Tea Party's collapse.

And this is not Riepen's only problem. Riepen has been forced out of *The Phoenix*, the new weekly alternative paper formed when *Boston After Dark* and the *Cambridge Phoenix* combined forces. The two had operated as inserts

to popular college newspapers on both sides of the river,
covering art, music, and politics in irreverent manner
that played like a more cordial, less crazed companion
to the recently shuttered underground papers *Avatar*
and *The Mole*. (*Avatar*, whose obscenity charges were
thrown out by the appellate courts, would be briefly
reincarnated as a national magazine before the Fort Hill
cult moved on from print to releasing a middling folk
album for Reprise Records.) *The Boston Phoenix*, as the
paper is now known, fills a gap between the underground
economy, the college economy, and the square economy.
The Boston Phoenix staff now rejects Riepen's leadership,
and he divests from the enterprise. Riepen's co-publisher
Richard Missner, buys him out after thirty staffers sign a
statement of support for Missner's leadership.

A similar battle is playing out in the 'BCN offices.
Riepen's business instincts—as valuable as they were
during the wild and wooly days—are now at odds with
the artistic vision of his employees and partners. His eye
for trends, his ability to see where businesses are going,
are at odds with the ideals of late hippie-capitalism.
His manner and management style are at odds with the
laidback anything-goes atmosphere of a radio station that
built its reputation on rambling monologues and oddball
tastes. 'BCN had begun to dictate the youth culture it
had once reflected and the way to wield that power is a
source of immense dischord. In the end, Riepen will cash
out and move on, but not before the station begins laying
wires to its Back Bay neighbors, a brand new recording
studio named Intermedia Studios.

On the last block of Newbury St., in an old, brick
Victorian on the southern side of the street, a few

hundred yards from the demolition and construction of the new Turnpike extension, Bostonians can find the latest in recording technology. Sixteen tracks of high-fidelity sound in rooms engineered to provide the best in audio separation, Intermedia is the first truly modern studio in the city. Despite years as a hub of musical activity—be it the classical students at the Berklee School of Music or the folkies in the coffee shops of Cambridge—the city of Boston has never been a hub of recording activity. From Barry & The Remains to Joan Baez, Bostonian musicians making the leap to the majors have almost always recorded in New York. Boston missed the explosion of recording technology in the wake of *Sgt. Pepper's Lonely Hearts Club Band*. Intermedia was founded to change all of that.

Led by Dr. Gunther Weil, entrepreneur and MIT educator, Intermedia's arrival in the Back Bay comes at an important moment in Boston media. The under-ground is consolidating. The underground newspapers are not so spacey. Advertisers expect more than rambling monologues and Moondog deep cuts from the city's progressive rock radio stations. Weil's focus on bridging the gap between album and demo recording and live broadcasts makes Intermedia a perfect extension of 'BCN's programming. Live concert presentations of the New York Rock Ensemble, Loggins & Messina, and Boz Scaggs have all been big hits. Weil has plans for television and film, too. Intermedia is cutting tracks for major and independent labels alike. Intermedia is filling a void at the center of the media landscape and the buzz is building.

When Jonathan Richman, Jerry Harrison, Ernie Brooks, and David Robinson walk through the doors at Intermedia, they aren't just entering the studio but entering a new phase of their career. The group know that a demo tape is the next logical step—they know they've got the sound, they know they've got the songs, but they want to be more than a local band playing local shows. With cash from performing high school dances and college mixers and the guidance of Stuart Love (a local scene fixture, talent scout, and promotions manager with Warner Brothers Records that ran in the same orbits as Danny Fields), the group cuts four songs in the studio: "Hospital," "Ride on Down the Highway," "Someone I Care About," and "Roadrunner." Four songs for the executives at the label to hear what this gawky teenager from deep in the suburbs has to say. Warner Bros. is on a hot streak since new label head Mo Ostin, a veteran of Frank Sinatra's Reprise operation, took over. Warner's acquisition by both the film company Seven Arts and the parking lot empire Kinney, have turned the label into one of the most powerful organizations in the recording industry. They are the label home of the Grateful Dead and Van Morrison. They have just bought Elektra Records from Jac Holzman, acquiring the catalogs of The Doors, The Stooges, and MC5.

But cutting an album and cutting demos are two very different things. A demo is a no frills recording, a simple straightforward document of unpolished material, raw and uncut. There were no overdubs, no ornate layers of sound to make the recordings sound lush and full. This is the sound of a mic in front of an amp, through a board and onto tape. Cut live, cut quick, a demo can have a dozen potential outcomes, from undreamt of success to unheralded failure. A demo is just as likely to never see the light of day as it is to start a career. A demo is just a sketch on a canvas. But sometimes it can be the start of something profound. As the tapes begin to circulate amongst the movers and shakers in the rock 'n' roll world, excitement sets in and word begins to spread about this wild new band from Boston.

Lillian Roxon: I don't suppose I would have ever got interested in Rock music, though I had been watching developments in that field for about a year because I could see how overwhelming a force it was going to be, but there are only two places to go at one in the morning. One was a restaurant near my home called Max's Kansas City, a place rock groups found comfortable, glamorous and convenient for late-night meals.[1]

Jonathan Richman: When I would sing "Roadrunner" the thing that would be going through my head would be of a cold freezing night out there. It was not cruising for burgers like American Graffiti, ya know, in a big car with a big engine. No, it was a lonely kid, which was me, in my father's station wagon all alone with just the white line—the little center, that passing lane thing, that white paint—and the dark blue of an ugly industrial park, Mercury Vapor Labs. Just this bleak lonely feeling. I never thought anyone would like that song. We put a good beat to it but I just thought how is anybody going to like this? I never thought anybody would.[2]

[1] Robert Milliken, *Lillian Roxon: Mother of Rock* (New York: Thunder's Mouth Press, 2005), 332
[2] *Jonathan Richman: Take Me to the Plaza*, 2003.

Lillian Roxon: Important footnote: I've just come back from Boston where I had my mind totally blown by a group called the Modern Lovers. They are not signed to a label (I can't imagine why it's taken the record companies so long) but their music is a kind of mixture of Velvet Underground, Kinks and the late Buddy Holly. Listening to 19-year-old Jonathan Richman sing "Roadrunner" is as exciting as listening to the early Velvets. Powerful, danceable, sinister and funny all at the same time.[3]

Lillian Roxon's importance in the rock pantheon cannot be oversold. Her *Rock Encyclopedia*, all six hundred and some odd pages of information on all the major players and mass movements that led to and sprung from the world of rock music, defined the canon. Before the *Rock Encyclopedia*, the idea of rock as a fine art was just a loose idea, a vaporous concept floating around in the ether. But the *Encyclopedia* proved that hypothesis. The *Rock Encyclopedia* is an heirloom-worthy tome that would give a generation of far-flung critics the vocabulary and history to make sense of a burgeoning culture. And this is just what Lillian does for fun, on nights and weekends, after work.

On the clock, she is an international correspondent covering the pop culture beat for publications across the globe. She'd gotten her start at a gossip mag in her native Australia before stops in London and Hollywood. She had taken rock music seriously before anyone in the mainstream media. She was beautiful and boisterous and

---

[3] Lillian Roxon, "Top of Pop: The Graceful Kinks," *New York Sunday News*, March 12, 1972.

an authority on what's cool. She is friends with Linda Eastman—who just married a Beatle—and Danny Fields, and anyone who is anyone in the rock establishment. She is the center of a swirling scene in the back room at Max's Kansas City. She is a rock 'n' roll oracle, a bridge between the old media and the new sounds. And she's got a column in the *New York Sunday News*, a paper popular with the suburban commuter crowd.

Back in Boston, a couple blocks south of the WBCN studios, across the bridge that spans the newly constructed Massachusetts Turnpike extension, a band named Aerosmith is practicing in the old Fenway Theater. The five piece—four friends that summered together in New Hampshire and a dropout from the nearby Berklee School of Music—had begun to carve out a niche in the city's rock scene. They are R&B fueled, aggressive, and clearly aim for popular success—the unabashed use of Rolling Stones' performance tropes being the biggest indicator. They've been barnstorming the hinterlands, playing boozy blues in no-name backwaters beyond Route 128 like North Reading, Massachusetts, Claremont, New Hampshire, and Brownsville, Vermont. They are building an audience, one high school auditorium, and college rec room at a time.

At Government Center, Kevin White is nursing an ulcer and a bruised ego after taking a drubbing in the race for governor. Despite big support from the Democratic establishment and an automated ad delivered to every household in Massachusetts via telephone—a bold new campaign technique untested in the Bay State—White couldn't muster the votes to unseat Governor Sargent. He could, however, muster the forces to get re-elected to the mayor's office. His assistant, a young savvy kid from New York named Barney Frank, has decided it is time to strike out on his own. Frank is running for the state house, representing a downtown neighborhood known as the Combat Zone, the last refuge of sin and vice now that Scollay Square had been knocked down and paved over.

Jonathan Richman: I wasn't anti-social, I was mostly narcissistic and into my own little thing when I was a 17, 18 year old kid. I was open to communicating but I was also sort of uptight and not very expansive. I would just walk up the street [being] critical 'ah, that place is no good, that's no fun. So I had a bad time but a lot of that is my own fault, which is how I hear a lot of that early stuff I did. When I'm listening, I'm hearing a kid who is having a bad time but a fair amount of it is his own fault.[4]

Ernie Brooks: Eventually someone—it must have been Danny Fields—called Lillian Roxon from New York Daily News *about the Modern Lovers. So Lillian came up and heard us play in this little dump and wrote about it for the newspaper—and that article started a sudden rush of record companies coming to see us.*[5]

---

[4] *Take Me to The Plaza*, 2003.
[5] "Jonathan Richman: In Love with the Modern World," accessed July 7, 2016, http://www.vice.com/read/jonathan-richman-in-love-with-the-modern-world

She Cracked

While it may not have been intended this way by the compilers of JojoChords.com, it is helpful to look at "She Cracked" as part of a triptych. Squeezed between the initial, frustrated contact of "I'm Straight" and the tragedy of "Hospital," "She Cracked" finds our narrator conflicted, confused as the object of his hard fought affection unravels before his very eyes. It is a classic second act, our hero having attained everything he wants, only to discover that his lover's self-destructive behaviors may be too much for him to handle.

From the first, urgent chords, it seems that Richman has finally met this match he has been looking for—she understands him, she's sensitive. They share things in common—she understands the old world, "the European things of 1943." They seem like a match, two souls aligned on a cosmic level but underneath you can tell something is wrong. The staccato organ and tight-wound bass riff warn that things might not be so stellar, discordance creeps in as the riff modulates, and then: She cracked.

She walked.

Our intrepid narrator has been abandoned, his hope for romance dashed against the pointed crags of the rock 'n' roll lifestyle. He saw it coming. We, the listener, may have even explicitly warned him that this was not going to work out. "You're right" he says (though he may also be speaking here to the specter of self-doubt, his constant companion in this arc of doomed desire). While there is a bond between the two, divergent appetites have driven them apart. The object of our narrator's desire is haunted, moved by unnamed trauma down a path of reckless consumption and dangerous behavior.

She self-destroys, Richman explains, to self-enjoy. He says it in a tone that is both sympathetic and condemning. She eats garbage, he continues, eats shit, gets stoned, as if to explain his disgust, to justify his need to break things off. Richman, transcendentalist that he is, stays alone, prefers eating health food at home, but is torn between his desire for love and the adherence to the principles of self-awareness and self-discipline.

Nowhere is that more clear than in the bridge where shards of discord scatter across the main riff like a broken bottle smashed against a highway sign at top speed. From there the song careens off course; drums, bass and guitar tumbling through sudden and atonal skronk, an audible illustration of the breakdown our narrator has witnessed first-hand. Capitulation to his flame's flaws would mean capitulating to the greater culture, becoming part of the broken system.

She cracked but he walked.

SPRING 1972: Starting a band is the easy part. Writing songs, playing shows, even the day-to-day tasks like hanging up fliers and maintaining a mailing list: those are the things that come naturally. The hard part comes when it is time to move up to the next level, when the time comes to find management and a label, to make the big moves it takes to get an album out into the world and into people's hands. When art meets commerce is where things get weird, when bankers and lawyers and the financial interests of corporations with quarterly sales quotas all come into the picture. It's like a game where three competing teams play different sports on the same field. Or a polyamorous relationship where each member of the relationship is actually a committee and each committee member has their own agenda and a long list of potential suitors just in case this specific courtship doesn't last. It is a very complicated, very convoluted process. And it doesn't help when an artist insists that they know what is best for their art. The record industry is not set up to make art the priority.

The Modern Lovers are very insistent about the importance of their art, confident that their sound, their style, and their inherent coolness were vital and unique. By the spring equinox of 1972, on the strength of Lillian Roxon's record label-scolding live review in the *Daily News*, the Modern Lovers are a hot commodity amongst the rock cognoscenti. That Roxon would travel hours outside of New York to the backwater of Boston to see a band nobody had heard of spoke volumes—she moves in rock's most elite circles, covers the biggest names in the scene. That she would compare them to her beloved Velvet Underground, a band that she helped canonize via their inclusion in her *Rock Encyclopedia*, said even more. Roxon is New York's top tastemaker, she essentially broke the idea that rock music should be given serious critical attentions, and record labels knew better than to ignore her enthusiastic exclamations. And even more than that, Roxon has an unfailing ear for great songs and an eye for cute boys.

The Lovers may still be playing small, self-booked shows but their audience increasingly began to include some of the music industry's most powerful figures. Clive Davis, head of Columbia Records and one of the industry's most powerful men, had shown up to a gig in a high school gymnasium in Cambridge. David Geffen, the industry trailblazer who had just launched the artist-friendly Asylum records, is poking around. A&M Records, the label founded by Herb Alpert and known as a bastion of creativity and commercial success, has expressed interest as well, even sending out a young A&R guy named Matthew Kaufman to meet the band. And Warner Bros. are still interested, maybe even more so now that they know their competition is interested as well. And Danny Fields, who has left Elektra records and joined up with Johnny and Edgar Winter's manager Steve Paul, is now looking to formalize a business relationship with the band after years of friendship and free advice. The band have options and leverage, a strange thing in a music industry where unsigned artists rarely occupy a position of power.

Over the course of the 60s, music industry power had slowly moved westward. Between L.A.'s studio-pop dominance and San Francisco's acid-fueled ascendency, California has wrested control from New York City and began to recraft youth culture in its image. Even East Coast acts like James Taylor, Bonnie Raitt, and Jonathan Edwards (of Bosstown also-rans Sugar Creek) had taken on the breezy smoothness of the Left Coast. Edwards' "Sunshine" is cruising up the charts, it is bright, hopeful, optimistic. It lacks the unstoppable restlessness of youth and unmovable weight of age. It is a song blissfully unaware of the world around it. Laurel Canyon hegemony is at its height and country rock is king in this small hip-industry enclave.

The Lovers arrived in California on the company dime. Two companies to be exact. In a rare move for the music industry, the suits at Warner and the suits at A&M see eye to eye and agree to split costs, each label getting the chance to walk the band through the old courtship rituals but only having to pay for half the date. And the band still doesn't have management. Kaufman has offered and Danny Fields and his new boss Steve Paul are interested but, still, no management; the band's sense of self-importance was making it hard to hand over control of affairs to an outsider. It makes this record label ménage á trois an even more impressive feat. When the Lovers arrive in California, they are bringing a markedly different energy with them and playing by a different set of rules. Stridently minimal and forcefully propulsive, the sound the Modern Lovers make in these California studios stands in stark contrast to the prevailing sounds of the West Coast.

The Modern Lovers' sound is diametrically opposed to the chart toppers and hit makers in A&M's stable. The label that Herb Alpert and Jerry Moss founded to release The Tijuana Brass' dulcet instrumental "The Lonely Bull" has become an industry juggernaut over the course of the 60s. Artists like Burt Bacharach and Liza Minnelli, Paul Williams, and The Carpenters are dominating AM radio. Rock acts like Free and Humble Pie were finding a home at progressive rock stations across the country. Joe Cocker, Cat Stevens, and Carole King are straddling both, creating a new niche of adult-oriented, rock influenced music that emphasizes the singer and the songwriter above all else. A&M are even the home of The Flying Burrito Brothers, who, with founding member and current Emmylou Harris collaborator Gram Parsons, helped make country music cool in the eyes of rock fans. When the Modern Lovers went into the studio to cut demos with Robert Apperre and Steve Mason, there was nothing like them on the label.

Warner Brothers Records' line-up was a bit different, assembled as it were through corporate mergers and label acquisitions in addition to traditional A&R work. From 60s veterans like the Grateful Dead, Frank Zappa, and Van Morrison to young stars of the 70s like Massachusetts-bred James Taylor and the ever-so-smooth Seals and Croft: that was Warner Bros. Their roster was stacked. Figure in their knack for ushering some of rock's heaviest acts out of obscurity—Black Sabbath, Deep Purple, and Alice Cooper all have big, new hit records out—and Warner Bros. seem like a good fit. But, most importantly, John Cale is working with Warner Bros. After two albums for Columbia—*Vintage Violence* and *The Church of Anthrax*, his collaboration with visionary composer Terry Riley—the former Velvet Underground viola player had signed with WB subsidiary Reprise Records as an artist and producer.

Both of the demo sessions are simple, mercenary affairs, quick sketches in preparation for a painting of a much grander scope. The Modern Lovers aren't recording an album; they don't have time to indulge in overdubs or an infinite number of takes. These recordings are fast, furious reproductions of the band as a live unit, snapshots of the living breathing thing that is the Modern Lovers, but there's a thickness of tone and nervous energy that didn't come through during the Intermedia sessions. The band sounds more confident, less overwhelmed by the studio environment, more comfortable battling back and forth like they do in the practice room. While the rest of Hollywood overdoses on punch-ins and studio tricks, the Modern Lovers are making rock 'n' roll the old fashioned way, four guys in a room doing it live, straight to tape. There is an energy, an immediacy, and vibrancy that has been increasingly marginalized since *Sgt. Pepper* ushered in the modern recording era. Tunes like the Cale-recorded "Pablo Picasso" and the Appere–Mason-produced "Modern World" explode out of the speaker like the band is playing for their lives. Slower numbers like the plaintive ode to monogamy, "Girlfriend," or "Astral Plane," Richman's poem to romantic projection, throb with tension and release, angst and naïveté. These recordings are a million miles from the polished and professional world of pop music.

The final death rattle of The Velvet Underground is hardly noticed by mainstream America. Despite ravenous fans flung from Boston to Cleveland to San Francisco, despite the support of the rock press luminaries like Lillian Roxon, Richard Goldstein of the *Village Voice*, and Lester Bangs at *Creem*, The Velvet Underground can't break out into the larger pop consciousness. They had been brought to notoriety by Andy Warhol, but when that relationship dissolved, the mainstream press stopped paying attention. They had jettisoned John Cale—the classically trained Welshman who had pushed the band into avant-garde territory—but that didn't push them into the Top 40. They had polished off the harsh edges, drawn back from extended noisy jams like the seventeen-minute "Sister Ray" and moved toward warmer, gentler songs like "Sweet Jane," but it was to no avail. And once Lou Reed had gone solo? It was a slow and inevitable slide into oblivion.

Not that Doug Yule doesn't try to make it work. He's jumped through all of the hoops that Lou had placed in front of him during the recording of the band's self-titled third album. He has pulled double during the sessions for *Loaded*, essentially filling in when his bandmates didn't show up, either by choice or by circumstance. Yule did his best to keep the band afloat. He even recorded *Squeeze*, essentially a Doug Yule solo record under the name The Velvet Underground just to keep the whole thing going. Sterling and Mo had left the band. They had even booked a couple of tours overseas with Walter Powers and Willie Alexander, two early Tea Party scenesters, taking advantage of the fact that Lou's departure hadn't been big news on other shores. It was a sad sputtering end for a band that had threatened to upend the entirety of rock 'n' roll culture.

Then, the Modern Lovers are back on the east coast and Steve Paul—Danny Fields' boss—wants the band to open a show for Edgar Winters, an audition of sorts to see how the band fairs in front of a big audience. The Edgar Winters' show is a disaster, not unlike the Tower of Power gig a couple months before and a few thousand miles away, where the West Coast horn-rock outfits fans had a vocal and violent reaction to the Modern Lovers minimalist agitations. The crowds on both coasts were hostile to the Modern Lovers. As beloved as they were in the elite circles of rock's upper echelons like the back room at Max's Kansas City, they are very vocally despised by rock's rank and file.

The propulsive minimalism of "Modern World" ain't gonna cut it when there's a room full of people anxiously anticipating the low-octane noodle-boogie of Johnny Winters' little brother or the big band funk of Tower of Power. Richman's earnest, honest longing wasn't going to be a crowd-pleaser when there was rock 'n' roll to be Hoochie Koo'ed. The Modern Lovers have a hard enough time winning over crowds at their own gigs on their own turf, but people that came to party with "Frankenstein"? They aren't going to flip their wigs for a song like "I'm Straight," with its talk of health food and sobriety.

The Edgar Winters' show marks the end of Danny Fields' involvement with the Modern Lovers. The Modern Lovers return to Massachusetts, no closer to having a record or management deal than they did before they left. They rent a house together near the coast, in a small town named Cohasset. They get back to the business of practicing, playing shows. Kim Fowley, Sunset Strip gadfly and oddball producer of outsider pop, comes through town not soon after. The Modern Lovers cut another demo, their third of the year, before Fowley leaves town. These demos bear all the hallmarks of Fowley's Sunset Strip aesthetic, a low budget version of the Joe Meeks/Phil Spector School of production, but hold little of the energy that made the West Coast sessions so vital.

Jonathan Richman: I never bothered to learn too much what the games were. I sort of—a whole lot of it I just never tried to understand. I just knew that I wanted to do what I wanted to do and if someone wanted to help me do what I wanted to do, great ... See, I had never heard of this idea of "takes". You did the song and that was it. And then the producer would say do it again. Do it again? What? Eat pizza for lunch? It's over. Someone says "we're gonna eat pizza again." Nah, we already ate lunch.[1]

*

Rolling Stone: Miss Christine's Story: She, too was born in San Pedro of Yugoslav parents. She was a "sickly kid,"she says, and had a "big complex about being skinny." (She is tall and lean, the type of girl who would have been called "beanpole" by her schoolmates.) "Pop music brought it all together for me socially," she said. "It brought people together, it gave me friends."[2]

FALL 1972: While you might not be able to tell based on reading the rock press—an old boys' club populated by new school freaks still steeped in machismo and male gaze despite otherwise progressive ethics—there are women involved in the music scene. Like Lillian Roxon, these artists, fashion designers, and free spirits help shape the visual and philosophical dimensions of rock, often with little or no acknowledgment of their contributions. Derisively known as "groupies," these women are far more than just sex objects, but partners in the aesthetic

---

[1] *Take Me to The Plaza*, 2003.
[2] John Burks, Jerry Hopkins, and Paul Nelson, "The GTO's," *Rolling Stone*, February 15, 1969.

development of Psychedelic America and its aftermath. Their influence is invisible but their impact huge; they are the travelers and documentarians that connect the pockets of rock deposited across the continent and across the globe. They are certainly more than "just a girl to bone" as Jonathan Richman might say.

The GTOs (Girls Together Outrageously) are, for all intents and purposes, the reigning queens of groupie-dom. Miss Pamela, Miss Mercy, Miss Cynderella, Miss Sparky, Miss Sandra, Miss Lucy, and Miss Christine are the coterie at the top of the rock pile. They are the women with access to the upper-reaches of the rock 'n' roll hierarchy, the women on the tour bus, the women backstage and at the hotel. They are as fearless and free as their male counterparts, bohemian hedonists who got hooked on rock music and made that culture the entirety of their lives. These women are rock stars and sexual revolutionaries in their own right, pop culture pioneers whose hipness shaped the cultural milieu. And, like Lillian Roxon, they love The Velvet Underground. Miss Cynderella even married John Cale.

When Miss Christine arrived at the Modern Lovers' rental house on the South Shore of Massachusetts she was a welcome guest offered a warm reception. Miss Christine was the devious genius behind the GTOs' first and only album *Permanent Damages*, the off-kilter out-of-tune rock record she and her friends had made with Frank Zappa. *Permanent Damages* lampooned and exposed the wild world of Laurel Canyon, mythologized the women that ran in the highest social circles of the rock and created a pop culture stereotype for better or worse. Miss Christine had been a nanny for Zappa's daughter Moon Unit. Miss

Christine was on the cover of *Hot Rats*, her voluminous hair creeping out of a concrete pool like some Hollywood space monster. When she was found dead the morning after her arrival, the affair was shrouded in mystery. Was it suicide? Was it an accidental overdose? Either way, Miss Christine had died at The Modern Lovers' house. She died a long way from San Pedro, spending only one night at the band's rental in coastal Cohasset, Massachusetts, before overdosing on prescription pills. The impact on the Modern Lovers as a unit is hard to measure. The shock of a sudden death amplified by the tensions of being broke, of being in each other's spaces all day every day as a tragedy unfolds: these are difficult things to quantify. But the darkness has arrived.

Frank Zappa: Christine was the one who recommended that I record Alice Cooper, and later provided them with ideas for their costumes. (When I first saw them, they looked pretty much like a bunch of guys from Arizona.)[3]

Miss Pamela: I was a homeless wonder, hanging out at Chuck's Cosmo Manor, when Mercy slashed her way through the sandalwood and found me in the den, writing to Marlon Brando. "Miss Christine is dead," she somberly announced through blackened tears. Her mascara had coursed down her cheeks in a splendid design, and I fixated on this while she gave me what little details she had been able to get out of Cynderalla.[4]

---

[3] Frank Zappa, *The Real Frank Zappa Book* (Touchstone, New York, 1989), 104.
[4] Pamela Des Barres, *I'm with the Band* (Chicago Review Press, Chicago, 2005), 259–60.

Hospital

She cracked but that is not the end of the story. "Hospital," the third installment of the story that started with "I'm Straight" and continued through "She Cracked," finds our protagonist regretful, apologetic for his harshness in light of her admittance to the hospital. He is conflicted, his feelings are stronger than his self-determination. Despite all of the rational reasons for abandoning his relationship, the idealist sees something worth saving. She cracked but he shouldn't have walked.

"Hospital" also marks Richman's return to the suburban-naturalism of "Roadrunner." The suburbs are dotted with relics of an earlier progressive era, stately buildings and landscaped grounds built to hide the shame of mental illness. McClane Hospital is the most famous—novelist Sylvia Plath and singer James Taylor both spent time in the Belmont psychiatric facility—but other psychiatric facilities are spread out across the state. These state hospitals are the darkness in the forest, the horror of which one does not speak.

Gone are the dervishes of "She's Cracked" and the motoring rhythms of "Old World" and "Roadrunner," replaced instead with an organ dirge, a funeral march for a love lost. The keyboard coos beneath a mist of guitar, raindrops of reverb falling on a gray New England day. There's a gentleness *that belies the fiery history of this relationship, that belies the turmoil roiling beyond the veil of the visible. When Richman sings that he's in love with your eyes, he is admitting that love is more than the confluence of habits between two humans. His understanding of the gaze and its power, that they need to see each other to understand each other, is countered by his own disgust at her behavior.*

Simply talking about the hospital, simply acknowledging that mental illness is real is an act of rebellion. Acknowledging the reality of depression and addiction runs counter-current to the stiff upper lip attitude that runs through the Bay State, it means admitting weakness. It means admitting that willpower and self-determination are not ends unto themselves. Our narrator, who has been stridently self-absorbed to this point, has begun to question the path of loneliness and idealism, and what Ralph Waldo Emerson referred to as "the extravagant demand they make upon human nature."

SUMMER 1972: This has been the craziest year of Kevin White's career. Since re-election as mayor of Boston, he has come within votes of being nominated as a candidate for Vice President of the United States on a ticket with George McGovern. His administration had secured the grants to restore Quincy Market and Faneuil Hall and helped bring the Inner Belt to a screeching halt. In just one night in July, he quelled two potential riots—one over police brutality in the Puerto Rican neighborhood, one a Rolling Stones show. He had to spring Mick, Keith, and crew from a cell in Rhode Island to prevent all hell breaking loose. It is a move that echoes his riot-preventing collaboration with James Brown in the wake of Martin Luther King's assassination. He is the rock star mayor, after all.

On Beacon Hill, Governor Sargent has declared a moratorium on new highway projects essentially ending the Inner Belt, the stretch of super highway running from Charlestown to Quincy that had already consumed entire neighborhoods in Allston and Cambridge. The neighborhoods had stopped the federal government: the people of the city stopped the relentless march of the bureaucratic juggernaut. A grassroots campaign, organized by the very people the Inner Belt sought to displace, had been heard in the halls of power. Their message has been carried all the way to Washington and back. The neighborhoods have survived.

The hole in Copley Square was on the mend. The hole has been reinforced, neighbors paid off for the structural damage the hole had caused. Now there is a building—or at least part of a building—stretching up from the hole, sixty stories of chrome rhombus bursting from the heart of the Back Bay. I. M. Pei, the same architects behind the desolate functionalism of Government Center, have designed a startlingly modern building: simple, sleek, and stunning, a shard of the future surrounded by a smattering of architectural trends from the prior two centuries. Compared to the dildo-shaped First National Bank Building in the Financial District, or the busy textures and space-age tropes of the Prudential Center, the John Hancock Tower is an architectural marvel, a triumph of the technocracy in Boston. But the windows keep falling out.

Big, coated, plate-glass windows that glisten in the sun, casting out rainbows of reflected light as they

THE MODERN LOVERS

plummet to the sidewalk. The building is said to wobble in a strong wind, someone along the way forgetting to take the aerodynamics of a chrome rhombus piercing the sky far above the city. The windows are becoming dislodged and there is no way to predict which one will dive to its inevitable doom next. The sealant that holds the windows into the frame, the sealant that allows the facade to appear as one gleaming surface stretching to the clouds, may not be strong enough to hold. The math could be wrong. The building could be twisting in the wind. The move-in day is pushed back again and the budget revisited.

In Government Center, the staffers at WRKO are celebrating a satisfying victory, enjoying their return to the top of the mainstream pack. Their crosstown rival, WMEX, the former home of hamburger slinger Artie Woo Woo Ginsburg, had started a programming war and lost. A DJ named John H. had taken over as program director at the number-two 'MEX and started hurling The New Music out into the universe, shifting playlists towards album cuts and listener requests, shifting the playlists away from the influence of record stores and sales figures. John H. made hits. He was into "Maggie May" by Rod Stewart before anyone. He says he was the one who told the label to release it as a single. He had tapped into the teen market but wasn't making headway in any other market. John H. had been let go and it was time to celebrate WMEX's return to the bottom of the ratings. Old ways can't be changed so suddenly in this town.

WINTER 1973: The New Year is off to a strong start in Boston. The Modern Lovers still don't have a label or a

manager, but they ushered in the New Year playing with
some of the hottest bands in the Max's Kansas City scene.
The New York Dolls, currently on the hunt for a record
label that isn't mortified by their cross-dressing stage
antics, invited the Lovers down to perform at Mercer
Art Center in Greenwich Village, the performance hall-
cum-practice space that was fostering the newest, most
radical music in town. Wayne County, who had been a
part of Jackie Curtis' ground breaking, gender bending
play *Femme Fatale* with a young poet named Patti Smith,
performed with his group Queen Elizabeth. The Magic
Tramps and Ruby & The Rednecks were on the bill too,
taking it out of regular show territory and into the world
of sleazeball cabaret.

Warner Bros. are still interested in the Lovers too.
Even though the band's brief jaunt to California in
early 1972 hadn't yielded enormous results—a couple of
demos, one disastrous gig with Tower of Power where the
audience were ready to turn violent by the end of The
Lovers' set—the label are still keen to make an album
with the Modern Lovers. So keen, in fact, that they
spring for a squad of industry types to fly out to Boston.
The Modern Lovers are opening up for Aerosmith,
who, after grinding it out on the same small-time rock
show circuit as Jonathan and company, have begun
their ascendency in the wake of their self-titled debut.
Aerosmith have built themselves a following, they've
got label support, radio support, and tour support, and
have Boston audiences eating out of their hands. This
wasn't another showcase in a strange town for a strange
audience; this was a hometown crowd. Rising tides and
all of that.

Rumor is Aerosmith payed to play at Max's Kansas City. Frank Connelly will tell you it was his connections that made it happen. The band would likely attribute it to their own talent. Either way they signed with Clive Davis and Columbia Records. Their self-titled debut was recorded at 331 Newbury Street, a couple of blocks from their old rehearsal space at the Fenway Theater. They were heading out on tour and the label had people working their sleazy Stones-isms to radio. Blues rock is ruling the day and Aerosmith were the masters of its most commercial form. It was the sort of musical marriage that dreams are made of. The drinking age has dropped to eighteen and there is an untapped market of teens that were ready to rage.

Jerry Harrison: When we got back to Boston, we tried, through the summer of 1972 and 1973, to decide what to do with all the offers. We were deciding between Danny Fields; working with Steve Paul; David Geffen with A&M; and then Warner Brothers, who flew in a whole raft of managers. We had opened for Aerosmith, and Warners and all the managers had gone out to dinner and missed our set. We had a huge basement in Arlington where we rehearsed, so we brought them all back there. David's father owned a liquor store and he got some liquor and we had an amazing concert. The managers thought we were fantastic. We interviewed each one for hours. We asked them what books they read and what they thought about this and that, but what we were really asking was what their morality was. We thought of ourselves as a cause and we didn't want to be ruined by something we thought would take away from the purity of what we were doing. Meanwhile we were destitudinally broke. We lived off record company dinners, which were once or twice a week. Once in a while, Jonathan's parents would visit. His father, who sold beef to army bases, brought along huge packages of Table Top pot pies and his mom brought a big fluffy sweater, which Jonathan had to put on.[1]

Boston Globe: "Remember that rock group I was telling you about last year," [Frank Connelly] opened, "and how all the record labels were interested?" Then, out from his greatcoat, he pulled out a record album. "Well here it is, their first album, for Columbia. It's called "Aerosmith" after their name. Columbia flipped when they heard the group." Then he whispered one of those confounded "off-the-record" items, an astronomical amount that Columbia paid to sign Aerosmith. "That's all I'm doing now: Managing the group and running this club, "Scarborough Fair" in Revere." Then Frank Connelly, whom Barnum would have loved, shook hands and zoomed out of sight.[2]

SPRING 1973: Bermuda is a long way from Boston, some six hundred or so miles in the middle of the ocean off the coast of South Carolina. Bermuda is an even greater distance away from the rock scene. The Modern Lovers are not the biggest band in town—that battle is currently being fought by Aerosmith and the J. Geils Band—and their fan club certainly does not stretch all the way to a tiny set of islands in the middle of the Atlantic ocean. That some brave soul said "Yeah, this band with the songs about being sober and lonely

[1] Scott Cohen, "Funny How Love Is," *Spin*, June 1986.
[2] Ernie Santosuosso, "Eyeing a Superstar-watcher," *The Boston Globe*, January 15, 1973.

and searching for answers *will work just fine for the early evening dinner show"* is tough to comprehend but alas the Modern Lovers are on an island in the middle of the Atlantic Ocean, playing for vacationers, booked between calypso bands. But the Modern Lovers are also broke and a tangential connection—a cousin of a friend—needs a teen act to play a resort. It's a match made in hunger.

The Modern Lovers have not left their troubles at home, however. The mounting tensions of living together, working together, traveling together, have followed the Modern Lovers from the mainland. The tensions that come from negotiating with bandmates, label execs, and one's artistic intuition followed the band from Boston to California and back again, and now those tensions had followed them to Bermuda. In the thirty-something months since Jonathan had formed the Modern Lovers, the stakes had sky-rocketed, there was money involved and contracts and a band couldn't just be a band. The Modern Lovers leaped from the fringes of a fringe scene, straight into the bubbling lava of the music industry volcano. Eruption is imminent.

Ernie Brooks: In the summer of '73 we went back [to California], *finally signed to Warner Bros., to record the real deal with John. After staying a while in Van Nuys at Emmylou Harris's place, we got this stucco house on Kings Road in Hollywood, one of those windy roads that runs off of Hollywood Boulevard, sort of hidden in the shrubbery. It was one of the scariest places because these houses were so isolated. One night we could hear the sound of helicopters circling, their searchlights trained on the house just down the road, and then we see the black cars driving up with guys with their sniper rifles and black vests—so we knew something was going on, but we didn't know what. We heard a lot of shooting and then cars driving away. There's something very sinister about LA that people don't usually talk about.*[3]

[3] "Jonathan Richman: In Love with the Modern World," accessed July 7, 2016, http://www.vice.com/read/jonathan-richman-in-love-with-the-modern-world

Someone I Care About

Here we find Jonathan returning from the isolation of the suburbs to the youth-heavy melee of modern urban romance. We don't know what happened to his hospitalized love interest, but "Someone I Care About" is devoid of any sadness and all softness is gone. Richman may be in pursuit of romantic love but he is no longer willing to accept compromise. He wants love but knows that it doesn't come for free. He is willing to pay the price for love but only if that person is worthy of love. The band concurs with a primal throb, propulsive and focused.

Richman is rationalizing loneliness, constructing a narrative in which he is no longer the unsure naïf pleading his case but the chivalrous hero relating tales of bravery. Richman is willing to sacrifice himself to the "28 misguided souls" looking to derail his date with malicious vagaries, willing to give himself up entirely for the love of the right woman. But in the milieu of the early 70s underground rock that woman was almost invisible, outshined by the overindulgence of the era.

"I don't want some cocaine sniffing triumph in a bar," Richman snarls, dismissing the substance that had become so prevalent in the post-psychedelic world of drug consumption. He doesn't want to get animalistic in the back of an automobile, either, and doesn't want to dehumanize anyone just for kicks,

a habit of the men in their ascendency to rock 'n' roll royalty. More than one frontman has exploited the sexual revolution for their own gratification but Richman wants all of us—his future girl, his listeners, himself—to know that he is not one of them.

When Richman sings "I don't want just a girl to bone," he denies the dominant narrative of heteronormative maleness. By admitting his desire for more than just sexual gratification, he breaks again with the dominant narrative in the rock 'n' roll mythos. Richman's idealism has returned, his confidence buttressed by experience. He is unafraid to seek an experience that is more than just sensual, more than just a series of temporary tingles to pass the time. He wants a girl to care about or nothing at all.

FALL 1973: At City Hall things are getting tense. The newspapers are raising questions about the hiring of Mayor White's father-in-law by the city-run Hynes auditorium. There is a constituency within the city that sees White's political ambitions—his ill-fated run for the Governor's Mansion, his near-miss Vice Presidential nomination—as a betrayal. There are folks that see it as a disinterest in the city of Boston. The gears of the old political machines are still turning and they have their sights set on the mayor's office and taking control of the vast, brick and concrete fortress in the heart of Government Center.

At Quincy Market, the Boston Redevelopment Authority is shaping the future of the refurbished market. There is little interest in the two-hundred-year-old market place, its old granite buildings, and aging, decaying infrastructure. Few people have attended the public hearings and nobody is protesting. For the BRA, this is a change from high visibility projects like the razing of West End. It is a quiet, little project compared to Government Center and the entire neighborhood they had to destroy to build a ghost town where no one ever goes of their own free will. Investors are quietly acquiring parcels on abutting blocks, preparing for properties to be part of the proposed retail and entertainment district in the places where sailors once rampaged on shore leave.

Nobody had predicted that, almost five years after breaking ground, the John Hancock Tower would still be vacant, still unfinished. These days, the windows on the first thirty-three floors are made of plywood, a temporary fix because there is still no consensus as to *why* the building has been hurling its chrome-finished, story-tall window panes smashing into the sidewalk. Were the windows too thick? Was it the insulation? The finish? The installers? The engineers? There are a lot of opinions being floated, by amateur and professional alike, but no definitive answer. The rumor mill says the tower is sinking—again—and another rumor says the building is going to be torn down, but in reality it is just going to sit empty for now. An empty chimera of plywood and glass stretching far above the skyline.

Boston Globe: The Sunset Series at Suffolk Downs concert Wednesday night was hopefully the worst concert to be seen there. The co-billing of Aerosmith and Sha-Na-Na drew a capacity crowd of rowdy, beer toting, preadolescents who should have been accompanied by a parent or legal guardian. As the sun set over the right side of the stage and clouds moved in from the west, Aerosmith began their set with "Make It."

Into the third song, a barrage of beer cans filled the air sending people to the ground seeking whatever shelter they could find. The show was stopped at least twice as Steve Tyler, pseudo Mick Jagger lead singer for Aerosmith, scolded the bubbly little teens, trying to make them behave. It didn't work and the show went on. Aerosmith is a local group catering to the bubble gum set. They put out a sound that will never grow away from the AM radio top 40.[1]

*

Ernie Brooks: [L.A.] that's where the problems started, almost immediately. I think it was because Jonathan had been changing. I don't think it was so much that he was getting tired of the old songs as he was developing this idea that the whole rock-'n'-roll-star-making machinery was corrupt. And part of that was the whole system of burning fossil fuels to generate electricity, using a lot of power for amps and sound systems, playing stadiums—you know, feeling that there was something wrong in profiting from all these things—and he started tying it all together in his mind and decided that he didn't want the Modern Lovers to be a conventional rock 'n' roll band.[2]

[1] Gary Lundquist, "Rock Review: Fans hit new low at Sunset series," *The Boston Globe*, August 3, 1973.
[2] "Jonathan Richman: In Love with the Modern World," accessed July 7, 2016, http://www.vice.com/read/jonathan-richman-in-love-with-the-modern-world

FALL 1973: The California sun shines brightly on the Modern Lovers as they bang out a set in the carport at Phil Kaufman's house. Kaufman, affectionately known as the Road Mangler, is a staple of the international rock scene, a rock 'n' roll adventurer and ex-con who had been Keith Richards' handler on some of the Rolling Stones' wildest tours. Kaufman has been assigned to the band by Warner Bros., a sort of last-ditch effort to keep tabs on the foursome who still had no official management, despite having signed a record deal earlier that summer. Kaufman is the Modern Lovers' Los Angeles liaison; he has scored them accommodations at Emmy Lou Harris' place. Kaufman also introduces the band to a former Harvard kid, former Byrd and former Flying Burrito Brother, Gram Parsons, who had become a fast friend.

And now, they are playing at Parson's wake. Well, not a wake in the typical sense. This is KAUFMAN'S KOFFIN KAPER KONSERT. Kaufman had promised Parson that if Gram died, Phil would take the body out to the Joshua Tree and burn it in a funeral pyre beyond the reach of civilization. And Kaufman did just that when an overdose took Parsons' life. Kaufman rode to the airport, abducted Parsons' coffin and rode off into the darkness. The trouble came not from the funeral pyre but from the funeral home, who considered the coffin to be stolen property and sent the L.A.P.D. out looking for the culprit. Kaufman was arrested, booked on grand theft and was bailed out broke and hard up for work: hence the KONCERT. Part wake, part fundraiser, the Modern Lovers' songs of loneliness and confusion provide a nice counterpoint to the gallows humor of Bobby "Boris" Pickett & the Crypt-Kickers.

This liminal existence is typical of the Modern Lovers in Los Angeles. Though they have a deal with a major record label they are not going to be the next Grand Funk Railroad. Though they are a band fueled by smart, concise songwriting they are not being lumped in with the Carole King–James Taylor-style singer-songwriters of the world. With their dressed-down, casual style they certainly aren't going to be adopted by the glitter rock scene that is currently swirling around Lou Reed and David Bowie. The Modern Lovers inhabit a psychic territory that seemed odd in the cold and grey of Boston, but in the bright light of the California sun seems downright bizarre. Their innate New England stoicism is softening and a meltdown is coming.

Studio success is evading the group. They signed with Warner Bros. because they wanted to record with John Cale, violist for The Velvet Underground and producer of The Stooges' records. The Lovers had recorded with him the last time they were on the West Coast. They had slammed through their live set and come out of the studio with pulsing, pounding versions of "She Cracked" and "Pablo Picasso." That first trip had resulted in a version of "Roadrunner" that bristles with bravado, that plainly captures four guys who have found *the pocket*— that mythical space where a group of musicians are perfectly in and out of sync. The versions of "Old World" and "Astral Plane" recorded on the last trip are transcendent, even if their presentation is straightforward and unrefined. But that magic is gone.

Cale and Richman are at loggerheads. Richman and the band are at odds. The label is worried. Art and commerce are at each other's throats. Volume versus dynamics. Darkness against light. Jonathan's restless creativity—the need to move forward that fuels songs like "Roadrunner" and "Pablo Picasso," the urges that had sent him out of the suburbs on a dérive to New York, Europe, and Israel before returning to Boston and starting the band—that creativity is taking him in a different direction from Cale, from the label, and from his bandmates. Jonathan, inspired by the calypso of Bermuda, and increasingly distasteful of high-volume performances, is moving in a softer direction. His tastes were regressing/progressing towards doo wop and the rock 'n' roll of the early 60s. The modern world was holding less sway over his artistic direction.

Cale, still infatuated with the Modern Lovers of '72, kept pushing for more anger, more aggression. Cale wanted the brute force that the Lovers had used to forge their sound, the conflagration of music that had made the band burn so bright. Day after day, take after take, argument after argument, the battle continues between two stubborn artists with radically different visions. The rest of the band is stuck on the sidelines, unsure of Jonathan's new directions and ready to finish the record they had worked so long and hard on. Instead, things with Cale sputter to a close, and the tapes are placed in the Warner Bros. vault, unheard by the world at large. But here in a carport in Phil Kaufman's backyard, the Modern Lovers are still making the rock 'n' rollin' modern sounds.

Ernie Brooks: [John Cale] *was growing increasingly frustrated with Jonathan and the whole ordeal. As I said, things weren't going great in Cale's life. One evening he even called me up and said, "I know my wife's there!" Of course, part of the story there was that she, Cindy, had been a close friend and bandmate of the GTOs' Miss Christine, who had died of an overdose the year before at the house we were renting on the South Shore of Boston, and that's another part of the story, of things that cast a pall over the Modern Lovers. Miss Christine's death had apparently totally destabilized Cindy.*

I said, "John, she's not here!"

I don't know what was going on, but I don't think it was good. I have to say, it must have been a terrible thing for Cale, because he was the producer of this potentially great record he wanted to make—that Jonathan wouldn't let him make—and at the same time we all admired him, but it just wasn't working out.[3]

Jonathan Richman: I would get testy with them if, like, I mean if record companies were interested. Ya know? We signed to Warner Brothers when I was about 21 or 20 or something and the rest of the band was 22. And they said "the rest of the band is in my office and they're upset." And I said "they are?" They went to the record office without telling me. And I said "why?" "Well, they say you won't do the song Roadrunner live." And I said, they're right. I might do it if I feel like it and I might not. "Well we've got to insist." Well you can come down and request it and I might or I might not. And they said well, "why should we support a tour?" Are you supporting a tour? "That's what the contracts say." Well then I'd rather go by Greyhound, if you're going to try and make me sing a song

---

[3] "Jonathan Richman: In Love with the Modern World," accessed July 7, 2016, http://www.vice.com/read/jonathan-richman-in-love-with-the-modern-world

then I don't want your tour. And that was the end of me and Warner Brother right there.[4]

The Boston Phoenix: Rumors indicate that this was to be the last Lovers band, with Richman either going solo or possibly, getting a new band together with Maureen Tucker of the Velvet Underground. The Lou Reed link is not accidental, because Richman's favorite band has been the Velvet Underground for many years, and he's seen them in concert 125 times at least. John Cale produced The Lovers' aborted album, so the Velvets influences are manifold in Richman's work though not determining its character totally. (Richman recently had a letter printed in Creem *magazine, knocking them for dismissing the tenderness of the old Four Seasons as "wimpoid".) And like all other acts under the Velvet mantle —Reed, Dolls, et al.—the Modern Lovers must be taken on their own terms.*[5]

[4] *Take Me to the Plaza*, 2003.
[5] Michael Bloom, "Music: The Last of the Modern Lovers?," *The Boston Phoenix*, February 19, 1974.

Girlfriend

The Modern Lovers have opened a portal into the future, have conjured a projection of what could happen where this dérive could take us. In this future Richman has found the girl to care about, the girl that isn't a part of the rock 'n' roll debauchery that swirls around him, the girl that understands both art and self-awareness and he is able to do something that he has never done before. At the Museum of Fine Arts in Boston, girlfriend at his side, Richman can see through the paint.

For Richman, the idea that love is the key to understanding art has been brewing since song one, side one. As Richman wanders the Fenway, heart in his hand, he sees beyond the medium, beyond the format to the greater truths that make important art transcend its own epoch. When he goes "to the room where they keep the Cezanne," he doesn't just see paint on canvas but the act of creation in a new context.

Richman's steadfast nature and self-searching have been rewarded with happiness and understanding. While he professes that he understands a girlfriend—G-I-R-L-F-R-E-N—the bigger implication is that the girlfriend understands him. Richman has struggled to convey his worth, his contrarian views often obscuring his erstwhile intentions. His distrust of drugs and self-destruction, his earnestness and empathy could

*all be hard to parse in the context and chaos of Boston's creative
community.*

*This vision of reciprocal love instills Richman's voice with
a newfound hope, an optimism and vitality that had long
been overshadowed by loneliness and distress. There is a sense
of relief and resignation that self-definition in the face of
overwhelming pressure from society was worth the hassle. In
this vision of the future, Richman and his Modern Lovers
have triumphed over the forces of hegemony. Love and understanding can occur beyond the confines of lysergic discipleship,
outside the hedonism that filled so many hollow hearts.*

*David Robinson: Jonathan was obsessed and we couldn't talk
him out of it. He wanted to play acoustic on street corners and
at rest homes, and I was supposed to play a rolled up newspaper
by banging my fist against it. I was the first to leave.[1]*

*Ernie Brooks: Jonathan started saying his old songs were too
negative and dark, and he started writing things like "Hey
There Little Insect," and maybe he was way ahead of us, but we
couldn't follow him—he wanted us to go, "Buzz, buzz, buzz"
on stage, but we were too cool!*

*We got about four crazy, not very satisfactory tracks done,
and then came the moment when Warner Bros. continued to
put pressure on us, which led to Jonathan saying, "Well, I'm
just not gonna do this anymore …"*

So Warner Bros. dropped us.

*So that was a turning point. It had gotten to where, if we
had something that people wanted to hear, Jonathan would*

---

[1] Scott Coen, "Funny How Love Is," *Spin*, June 1986.

*refuse. It was a conceptual way of approaching rock 'n' roll—
but not a way to make a living or feel very happy.*[2]

1974: Jonathan Richman is at home, singing into a tape
recorder. He sings new songs, and old songs, and half-
finished songs, and songs that may not have existed
before they escaped from his brain to the tape. His songs
are simple, scaled back, tender, and delicate. This is not
the primal pulsing throb that John Cale had tried to coax
out of Jonathan in California. These aren't the straight-
ahead rock songs that Warner Bros. wanted. These aren't
the hits that the rest of the band thought they were
creating. These are new, stripped down, almost a retreat
to a mythical time before the amplification wars of the
late 60s. These songs stretch back to a world of doo wop,
rock 'n' roll, to a childhood that may or may not have
existed. These songs mark a new direction.

The band has split and Jonathan is searching for that
next sound. Jerry Harrison has gone back to school,
studying architecture and contemplating his next move.
David Robinson is returning to L.A. to join a band
named The Pop, which may be both a description and
an aspiration. Ernie Brooks is back in Boston, playing
in pick up bands here and there. The Modern Lovers
Mach 1 are over, the fractures between frontman and
sidemen, frontman and producer, frontman and label,
just too much to work through. They had flown too
close to the sun, their waxwings melting in the heat of a

---

[2] "Jonathan Richman: In Love with the Modern World," accessed
July 7, 2016, http://www.vice.com/read/jonathan-richman-in-love-
with-the-modern-world

California summer. They had burned bright and burned fast, flaming out before most of the music world was even aware they existed.

But this new tape holds promise. The half-formed songs and half-improvised poems will never be confused for arena rock, even once polished and shined. This tape showcases a limber mind freed of constraints and expectations. The tensions and worries of the earliest Richman material, his loneliness and need for love, the desire to be accepted and the fear of rejection that defined The Modern Lovers as a musical unit, were supplanted by new fascinations, new concerns. As Richman hams it up for the microphone, speaking to an audience that will be scattered across time and space, you can hear a new joy has filled the vacuum where that old New England cold and bitterness once was.

Richman and his newest recording are as far from the music business as one can get—physically, mentally—and you can hear renewed energy in both the songs and the singer. And though distance from the industry has increased, interest from the industry has not. Matthew Kaufman, who has been offering to manage Jonathan since A&M Records' earliest dalliances with The Lovers, is still in communication. Kaufman's got a new project in the works, a new label with new bands and a new sound. Kaufman is fully aware of the flame out at WB, the battles fought over the artistic direction of the band and the album unfinished in their vaults. But Kaufman is still interested, still in communication.

Rock is serious business. Gone are the days of anarchy and marginality. Rock has moved out of the makeshift spaces and oddball venues into the serious rooms of the city, the theaters, the arenas. The drinking age had dropped to eighteen and the city had sprouted clubs and performance rooms in every darkened corner. Kenmore Square, on the other side of the Turnpike extension from The Tea Party's second home, has become a hot spot. Catering to the Boston University crowd and the influx of young people still pouring into the city, long after the Battle of the Boston Common was fought and lost, Kenmore Square is the city's newest nightlife hub. Lucifer is on the north side of the street, four floors of decadent dancing. There are bars with folk, blues, jazz pouring music onto the street every night of the week. And in the basement of 1314 Commonwealth Avenue, in the Rathskeller Lounge at Old Vienna Hofbrau (the kids call it The Rat) you can find new music from some familiar faces.

Dischord has come to the newsrooms of the city's weekly newspapers. Stephen Mindich—owner of *The Phoenix*—is going before the National Labor Relations Board, battling over the writers' rights to unionize. The politics of the ledger sheet and the politics of the editorial page are at odds; pay is being disputed. The paper is slinging between 80,000 and 100,000 copies a week, raking in an alleged $1.8 million in ad sales last year. The writers at *The Phoenix* and its crosstown rival have an immense influence on the youth culture of Boston, but their pay is incommensurate. It is a fight as old as journalism itself, one that the writers often find themselves losing. But it seems especially incongruous with the alternative identity the publications are trying to project. Alternative culture is big business, whether or not the culture is willing to admit that.

Aerosmith's sophomore album *Get Your Wings* is a much bigger record than the band's self-titled debut. While it isn't denting the pop charts the way the band or the label would like, *Get Your Wings* marks a significant move forward from their prior LP. The band left Boston to record, heading to the Record Plant in New York rather than sticking with Intermedia Studios in Boston. They have teamed with Jack Douglas who turned the knobs on the first New York Dolls record and has just finished the new Alice Cooper record. The band had toured the country repeatedly, done all of the promotion a young band is expected to do, but still couldn't connect with the gatekeepers in the rock press. While rock culture may have solidified its position as America's dominant cultural trope, there is still this sense that Aerosmith are too commercial for their own good, their approach too calculated. Or not calculated enough. With three singles bubbling under the charts, lukewarm reviews and critical indifference plague the band even as their reputation for wild live shows grows.

The J. Geils Band's fortunes are looking better, however. After releasing two albums in 1973, *Bloodshot* and *Ladies Invited*, and landing a couple of singles on the radio, the band have returned to the Hit Factory in New York. Years of hard work and hustle have resulted in one of their hardest, funkiest studio albums to date, *Nightmares ... And Other tales from the Vinyl Jungle*. Produced by Bill Szymczyk, who recently helmed the Eagles' mega-hit *On the Border*, *Nightmares* puts an East Coast spin on New Orleans vibes. *Nightmares* makes for one serious party. "Musta Got Lost" has found a home on radio, its woozy love-drunk exhortations connecting across the country.

Nixon's office has barely been vacated and there's already talk of Kevin White running for president. It's two years out and there are certainly obstacles in the way—including the juggernaut Kennedy clan— but White has never lacked for political ambition. His management style has changed since the early days: less delegation, more direct orders. He canned the head of the rent control association, who had a reputation among landlords as being too pro-tenant. White is gutting the Boston Redevelopment Authority, shaking up the power structure and reining in its influence.

Boston Globe: Too much sameness, creatively pale was my assessment of that first undertaking by Aerosmith. I wasn't about to liken his posturings to those of Jagger, without having seen the act, so that wasn't a factor. "Get Your Wings" is their second release and while I don't consider Aerosmith one of my favorite five or six rock groups I have altered my evaluation of their playing considerably upwards. An evident maturity has set in, this is obvious from a collection of discipline performances, several intricately structured and ably navigated.[3]

---

[3] Ernie Santosuosso, "Aerosmith Album has Wings," *The Boston Globe*, April 21, 1974

Modern World

And then, all of a sudden, bam-bam, we shift gears. The Modern Lovers grab the listeners' hand and pull them back into the present, back to the modern world. It's not so bad, Richman says nonchalantly, not like the students say, intoning that he's over the strife and discourse and protest for protest sake. The band are moving forward, guitar solos propelled by strident hand claps, keyboard pushed beyond breaking point, verses and choruses flying by like trees along the highway.

Richman returns to familiar territory, to the pride in place we felt radiating from "Roadrunner". When he sings "I'm in Love with the U.S.A." it is not simply knee-jerk nationalism, not "Ballad of the Green Berets" type militancy, but genuine love for the place that has made him, shaped him with all its triumphs and faults. There's sex in a sunny day, that shines down on Boylston Street, Richman tells us, enticing us to bask in the glow of brand new buildings that reach into the sky, seducing us into a love affair with the progress we cannot stop.

Stop all this weak stuff, Richman moans. Drop out of BU, Richman pleads. He is imploring his audience to rethink their adherence to societal norms—to college, to cigarettes. Route 9 may be bleak and nearly dying once you get to the city limits but beyond that there is beauty. There is beauty beyond the decay and excitement outside in the real world, in the modern world. "Modern World" is when Richman makes a break with the affectations of hipness, the distance and detachment Americans have used as the yardstick of cool for a generation, maybe more.

The Modern Lovers have become what Ralph Waldo Emerson called "collectors of the heavenly spark with the powers to convey that electricity to others." "Modern World" makes the case that nostalgia and nihilism make a distasteful pairing, that being closed off to new experiences does not make you cool. When the band sing back "I love the U.S.A." they are taking a stand against waves of darkness that were threatening to envelope their generation.

1975: Investigations are being opened into whether the Mayor's office is commanding its employees to vote for their boss. The city's Financial Committee has begun investigating the administration's use of funds. The Fire Department has become a focal point of fury for its hiring practices and internal politics that reek of the old machines and the clannish corruption that defined the dirty Old Boston that came before this administration.

White has forced Police Commissioner Robert DiGrazia out of his position, a move that pundits speculate is preempting another corruption investigation. There's also talk that the position was opened up so that White could give it to Boston Redevelopment Authority director Robert Kenney and replace Kenney with a bureaucrat more amenable to White's orders. With the stroke of a pen he shuts down the "Walkway to the Sea," the pedestrian bridge intended to erase the increasing danger of the crossing beneath the Central Artery that connects Government Center to the Waterfront. Well-intended but short-sighted, the walkway is endemic of Boston's long-running approach of pouring concrete over problems rather than dealing with them directly.

In the Back Bay, problems can't be fixed with poured concrete. The John Hancock Tower still isn't open. The windows still haven't been entirely replaced, with full floors covered in plywood as thin panes are traded out for thicker panes. But that is an old problem. These days the worries are about the entire tower collapsing in the event of cataclysmic winds. While the engineers were solving the window problem, they discovered that the building's design, its rhomboid shape and smooth facades reaching to the sky, wouldn't hold in high winds. Braces are being installed internally, to combat the twisting and the swaying that could shred the very structure of the tower. Four years' late and tens of millions of dollars over budget, the John Hancock Tower sits empty, covered in plywood like a burnt out building.

A few blocks north, WBCN is still the city's number two FM station, right behind perennial ratings champ and "beautiful music" titan WJIB. 'BCN's success has become a model for others, a national tastemaker, and a guiding light in Boston's radio community. WCON, the distant, beleaguered competition to WJIB, has abandoned its beautiful music format for the 'BCN-lite *modified progressive* format. On the AM dial, WMEX and WRKO are in stasis, as FM becomes the dominant format of the day. WMEX has rehired Arnie Woo Woo Ginsburg, the hamburger-slinging hero of Boston's early Top 40 era after eight years as a journeyman manager, including a two-year stint as 'BCN GM in the waning days of Ray

Riepen's run as owner. The AM dial has become increasingly album oriented, its pull with younger fans waning as FM rock becomes the dominant force in popular music.

Across the river, in a basement at MIT, a young man going by the name of Oedipus begins broadcasting the latest in underground sounds at 88.1 FM WTBS. Oedipus' show is becoming appointment listening for young, adventurous music fans craving a cultural counterpoint to the big, boorish sounds farted out by the other end of the FM dial. Oedipus has an ear for the raw, the avant-garde, the anarchistic, the rock 'n' roll outsiders. Oedipus is one of the first to realize that a new music is forming, a reaction to the Edgar Winters of the world. There is a new musical force that picks up the mantle for The Velvet Underground, The Stooges, the MC5. Late into the night at the far left side of the dial, the road map to rock's new directions is being drawn.

Jonathan is recording again. He has returned to California to work with Matthew Kaufman, who had been offering assistance since the very earliest days of the Lovers' major label courtship rituals. Kaufman has left A&M to start his own label, Beserkley Records. "The Home of the Hits" is the tag line, a self-effacing announcement that the label isn't shying away from its pop aspirations. Kaufman is recording a compilation, the audaciously titled *Chartbusters Vol. 1* and wants to work with Richman. Kaufman is even providing the backup bands—Beserkley labelmates The Rubinoos and their compatriots in Earth Quake—since Richman is a solo artist these days, using pickup bands for occasional gigs. Things are looser these days. Jonathan even picked up a gig as a drummer for a night, backing up New York poet

Patti Smith and *Fusion* writer Lenny Kaye for a one-off at the Fillmore West.

Things are different this time out. The studio isn't a battleground. Kaufman is more open to Jonathan's new ideas, his new direction, than John Cale was during the Warner sessions. The passion is there but the volume is turned down. The energy is there but the dynamics are broader, the palette of tone colors bigger. The tension and angst that bristled through earlier recordings of "Roadrunner" have dissipated. The instruments and instrumentalists are battling for attention. The version of "Government Center" bursts with positivity and joy, eclipsing even the happiest moments of the Kim Fowley recorded cut. The *Chartbusters*' version of the Modern Lovers—Modern Lovers Mach 2—is bright, boisterous, beaming positive energy out into the world. "Roadrunner" brims with optimism, bubbles over with freedom and joy. The distortion is dialed back. The primal throb is a little more sophisticated. There have been a lot of detours along the road to Jonathan Richman's first appearance on vinyl but the journey has been well worth it. The old New England Bitterness is gone.

John Cale's cover of "Pablo Picasso," from his sixth solo record *Helen of Troy*, certifies that the song is an underground hit. Even though the album was never released and the tapes are languishing unheard in Warner's vaults, "Pablo Picasso" is the sort of song that burrows into the listener's brain and stays there. That Cale would return to it, that it would be a natural fit for The Velvet Underground member's solo oeuvre is obvious. His original demo, recorded in California under strange circumstances back in

1972 had surfaced on Beserkley's *The Modern Lovers* compilation, adding to Cale's cache as a progenitor of the aesthetic that was becoming punk rock. The song's brusque talk about assholes and brutish behavior is a perfect set-up for Cale's hard heavy wah-pedal rework of the Lovers' two-chord masterpiece. The master–student relationship is refracted and repurposed, the nature of influence warped and redirected to create the model for the next wave of students and masters. Cale is an apex tastemaker, a man whose influence runs deep and runs wide. His inclusion of "Pablo Picasso" puts Richman's work on the stereo of art-rock fans all over the world.

Boston Globe: "When I was 14," [Steven Tyler] *confesses, "I got busted for pot. Three months later I got busted again in Florida. Politics means trouble, which is why I stay away from politics and don't give it any thought.*

"What I dig is money. It pays for things. I'd like to buy myself a Porsche. I already own a ChrisCraft, and I just bought 159 feet of lakefront property in Sunapee."

Aerosmith seems to stimulate audiences and many fans have been injured at their performances, which is also true of the Bay City Rollers in England.

To date Aerosmith has three gold albums, "Aerosmith" and "Toys in the Attic" and "Get Your Wings," to their credit. And their star is rising rapidly. Are they representatives of today's youth? Surely they represent one segment of it.[1]

---

[1] Pamela Swift, "Keeping Up … With Youth," *The Boston Globe*, November 16, 1975.

Toys in the Attic is the breakthrough Aerosmith has been working towards. After years of grinding it out in weird backwaters and fringe markets, clamoring for attention from critics and consumers alike, Aerosmith have finally hit the big stage. Radio hasn't latched on but the songs are tailor-made for the arenas that Aerosmith play as an opening band. The songs are big and unsubtle, brash declarations of boozed-up bravado, background music for plebeian debauchery. Aerosmith have become the outsized rock 'n' roll personas they had always tried to project. They have become the myth of Aerosmith. They have become rock stars.

The J. Geils Band are right behind them. They are releasing another live album, their last for Atlantic, the final record of their contract. The album does well, but the songs aren't gaining the same traction on the radio that they were just a year ago. As always, the Geils' live shows are rowdy affairs, part revival meeting, part cartoon explosion. The way Peter Wolf and company rile the crowd is nothing short of ecstatic. But something needs to happen if the band are to keep growing, something needs to bridge the gap between live performances and the recordings.

Back in Kenmore Square, on the other side of the Turnpike opposite Fenway Park and the old Boston Tea Party, there's a noise coming from the basement of the Old Vienna Hofbrau. John Felice, original Modern Lover and longtime friend of Jonathan Richman, is playing there with his new band The Real Kids. Willie Alexander—known as "Loco" in music circles has formed the Boom Boom Band following his short run with the doomed Doug Yule-led incarnation of The Velvet

Underground. Ben Orr and Ric Ocasek, who'd rode the wave of Boston singer-songwriters in the early 70s to an ABC Records contract with a band named Milkwood, are working on new material under the name Cap'n Swing.

Dignified and Old

By "*Dignified and Old*," *Jonathan Richman's vision—of himself, of love, of the world around him—has expanded, his perception has widened beyond the suburbs, beyond the frustration of reciprocated love. He is alone in the desert—be it literal or metaphorical, it doesn't matter—and he has arrived in the place where 20th century prophets and heralds discover the next path they must follow. No girl understands me, he says into the vast barren wilderness, but I can see through this bleakness.*

The debilitating loneliness that had driven Richman to the astral plane, the need for connection that drove him to call the object of his affection to make the case against Hippie Johnny, the loneliness that had driven him out to the highway late at night, has ceded to some new territory. Richman can now see that loneliness and sadness should not be the defining characteristics of his existence. He wrestles with his hopes for the future, his friends say he contradicts himself, but he realizes that this is all part of the process of growth.

Vision and momentum are so essential to the Modern Lovers sound that eventually they would propel the band beyond the concerns of youth. Richman has made his break with the prevailing attitudes of the American Cult of Youth.

He has realized that his fate lies beyond the orgy of post-adolescent consumerism and that there is more on the table than immediate thrills and instant gratification. Oh, I can take a challenge, Richman proclaims, and so I won't die.

Richman knows it; he knows that he'll be dignified and old. It is the same sureness that drove him to perform on the Cambridge Common. It is the same sureness he had when he told Danny Fields he wanted to be a rock star. The same sureness that tells him, if he had a girlfriend he would be able to look through the painting. In the face of rock 'n' roll's wanton self-destruction, amidst the wave of early deaths that had decimated the ranks of those psychedelic pioneers, Richman is going to be the one that transcends the youth cult to become dignified and old.

When the rest of the band responds to Richman's call of "hey kids," there is a sense of resignation, a tinge of disappointment that for all the power and magic of rock 'n' roll, it still can't stop the march of time. But there is also a feeling of optimism, that all of the trials and tribulations, depression and disappointment will have been worth it. Death and sadness are not the end—there may be darkness now but the light is coming. One day, Richman sings, we'll be dignified and old together.

Sounds (U.K.): Alright, so perhaps I am going just a weeny bit over the top with the 10 star rating up there, but the fact is at the moment I'd rather be playing this little platter than anything else. And if you're of the same opinion as myself that Mr. Jonathan Richman's "Roadrunner" was the '45 of '75, then I wager you'll get as crazy over TML as I am ... Anyway, for those few with the ears to hear it, "Roadrunner" and its LP companions, "New Teller" and "Government Centre," constituted instant classic material. Richman sounded like a younger, slightly more adenoidal Lou Reed, and his songs had the pump and grind of early Reed classics like "Run, Run, Run."[1]

1976: Rare is the artist who can claim two debut albums in the same year, much less two debut albums released within weeks, but Jonathan Richman has never been a typical rock 'n' roller and The Modern Lovers have never been a typical band. His collaboration with Matthew Kaufman and Beserkley Records was proving fortuitous. A single had been released for "Roadrunner" (with "Government Center" on the flipside) which hadn't charted but had found attentive ears in the music press. *Chartbusters Vol. 1*, the compilation Jonathan appeared on with Earth Quake, The Rubinoos, and Greg Kihn, had found its way into the hands of serious pop fans. College radio shows like Oedipus' on WTBS are latching on to the urgency and immediacy—and unshakable hooks—Kaufman had elicited from his groups. *Chartbusters Vol. 1* sounds like the crest of a new wave in American music, an extension of 60s pop songcraft, all hooks and singalongs and infectious melodies, with a keen sense of self-awareness. It is as much a snapshot of a sound and sensibility as it is a sales sampler. *Chartbusters* is a testament to the power of pop.

Kaufman's belief in Jonathan, as a performer and an artist, has opened up new directions in the young Natick native's songwriting. The dynamic is different with Jerry and Ernie gone. David Robinson has returned from his run in L.A., but the volume is lower, the distortion gone.

[1] Giovanni Dadomo, "Jonathan Richman and The Modern Lovers: The Modern Lovers," *Sounds*, July 3, 1976.

Over the course of pick-up gigs and lineup tweaks that have brought Curly Keranen from The Rubinoos and Leroy Radcliffe into the fold, the power and amplitude of the Modern Lovers had been reduced to nothing. The wailing assault of The Velvet Underground "Sister Ray" had been all-but stripped from the Modern Lovers' sound, replaced with the playful gentle sound of tunes like "I'm Sticking With You." The sound returns to the other side of the 60s, a sound that predated the escalation in amplification that had bands like Aerosmith hiring tractor trailers to cart their sound equipment from one city to the next. The new sound of the Modern Lovers was brighter, lighter, looser. This new incarnation of the Modern Lovers could tour in a hatchback if they had to. They could take a Greyhound from gig to gig if need be, just acoustic instruments and handclapping. By the end of the summer, they have a debut album, *Jonathan Richman & the Modern Lovers*, out on Beserkley.

Mach 1 of the Modern Lovers, however, hasn't been forgotten. The tapes from the early demo sessions are being passed around, the way all the best music usually is, copies of copies from fan to fan. They've made it to London, where the last manager of the New York Dolls, Malcolm McLaren, owns a clothing store named Let It Rock. The tapes have made it around New York, where a new band named Talking Heads have worked up their own version of "Pablo Picasso." Even though the band has been dissolved for almost two years, their popularity keeps growing. The reputation outstrips the distribution, the band's brilliant and brief conflagration taking on more mythical proportions with each retelling. The band's rebellion against the record labels, the band's insolent rejection of hippie culture, the band's inability to cave to commercial concerns strike a chord with music fans who feel alienated by the greed and consumption of the arena rock era. The band's legend growing every time the mantra of Radio On! passes over the tapeheads. Matthew Kaufman, hip listener he is, knows that those words contain magic. He makes a move.

The Modern Lovers is as austere and elegant as a rock 'n' roll album can get. Eight songs cherry-picked from the first round of California demos—the ones that were cut fast and live, six of which are John Cale productions—and "Hospital" from the very first trip to Intermedia Studios on Newbury Street. From the count-off of "Roadrunner" to the closing notes of "Modern World," *The Modern Lovers* creates an alternate universe where *White Light/White Heat* was bigger than *Sgt. Pepper's* and the world is overrun with over-driven electric piano. The Modern Lovers expand the canon of the burgeoning rock underground cultivated by fanzines like *Punk* in New York, *Who Put The Bomp* in Los Angeles, and *Boston Groupie News* back home. Too cool for their own time, the songs on *The Modern Lovers* appear in the popular consciousness at just the right moment to predict and participate in a cultural moment.

Jonathan Richman: That demo with "Roadrunner"? Yeah, it came out in about 76 and I was already into much different stuff by the time. The guy who bought the tapes ya know said "can we release this stuff?" Cuz he owned Beserkley Records and I was recording for them. And I said "I guess if you want to" but I wasn't thrilled with the idea. I didn't even consider it my first record, to me it was just a bunch of demo tapes, but I said oh okay. So he released all those things which to me were just old history.[2]

Melody Maker: Still, the debut stands head and shoulders above his other work. It's an astonishing piece of vinyl, which effortlessly transcends the interminable Reed/Stooges/Doors comparisons. As Brian Wilson had his finger firmly on the pulse of West Coast surfarma during the Sixties, Jonathan distilled the whole gamut of US tear-dream imagery, hopes, fears, frustration, rejection, pain and confusion for the seventies.

His infatuation with and understanding of the music's essence harks further back to the embryonic daze of rock 'n' roll when people like Elvis, Chuck Berry, Carl Perkins and Eddie Cochrane were frantically trailblazing.

Before their metaphorical death, they managed to fuse strong, original material, imaginative playing and sharp—while still improvised—vocals in a sound that was simultaneously tough, tight and bursting with life.[3]

SUMMER 1976: Now in his third term, Mayor Kevin White has wrested control of most city operations from the department heads who had been running their own private empires for years. The corruption investigations of 1975 had turned up nothing on White—and hardly slowed his re-election—but they had brought up questions of oversight and the Mayor's ability to govern. The Mayor is still entertaining thoughts of national

[2] *Take Me to the Plaza*, 2003.
[3] Ian Birch, "Jonathan Richman: In Love with the Modern World," *Melody Maker*, September 17, 1977.

political office, his perceived wanderlust a detriment in the eyes of his detractors.

But there have been some successes: Quincy Market, the restoration undertaking that had been White's pet project since LBJ was in office, is finally open. The vendor stalls are filled with alluring sights and smells, the two-century-old building refurbished and repaired after years of neglect. The adjoining buildings, North Market and South Market, are being remodeled too. Investors have begun buying property on the waterfront. There is again talk of tearing down the Central Artery, which runs alongside the Market District, and replacing it with a tunnel under the city. It will be a big dig, but worth it.

In the Back Bay, the John Hancock Tower has opened its observation deck. Eight years after breaking ground, the John Hancock Tower is now home to one of the city's best views and one of the nation's tallest office buildings. After eight years of collapsing neighborhoods and shattering windows, emergency wind braces, and a $125 million price tag, the John Hancock Tower is open: 790 feet of mirror shooting into the sky, piercing the atmosphere far above this ancient American city, dwarfing its neighbor the Prudential Center by more the ten stories. And for a dollar fifty you can ride to the top and see from Cape Cod's northernmost point to Southern New Hampshire.

Across the Atlantic, punk rock is exploding onto the British charts. The Sex Pistols, the band formed by New York Dolls manager Malcolm McLaren, is cursing, and spitting, and snarling their way into the popular consciousness. The Ramones, the new band that Danny Fields is managing, are releasing their debut and storming both sides of the Atlantic with a high-energy blast of mutant bubblegum pop. The Ramones' compatriots at the New York city club CBGB—the heir to the legacy of Max's Kansas City—have become the locus of a new media storm. Blondie, Dead Boys, and Talking Heads are turning heads at record labels and in magazines. The underground that had been simmering just below the surface since the days of the Velvets and The Stooges was now nipping at the heels of the mainstream. From L.A. to Paris, the world was awash in the primal throb.

Back in a sweaty, sticky basement club in Kenmore Square known as The Rat, across the turnpike extension from Fenway Park and the cavernous, old Boston Tea Party, a tape is rolling on Boston's own punk rock insurgency. *Live at the Rat* is the definitive document of a definitive moment. When Willie Alexander, who had played the opening night of The Tea Party as a member of The Lost and who'd toured in the end-days line-up of The Velvet Underground, belts out the opening notes of "Mass Ave." it's like the city had been absolved of all its soft rock-singer sins and born anew, baptized in the divine waters of rock 'n' roll.

Contributions from John Felice's The Real Kids, DMZ, and Thundertrain are primal, mutant rock 'n' roll, each different enough from the next to make one realize that there is no sound. There never was a sound. The strength of a music scene doesn't come from sameness, from duplicity. The strength of a music scene comes from diversity, from the interaction of different ideas from different origins. The energy, the tension, the anxious edge of a city filled with kids, free from the constraints of the old world, is finally captured on tape.

Aerosmith have transcended the Boston scene, entering the nether world of rock superstardom. They finished '75 as the top selling artist on Columbia Records. Their fourth album *Rocks* is a paean to transgression, a set of sleaze-by-numbers rawk tunes that simultaneously finds the band at their most crass and most commercial. "Rats in the Cellar" gets low, gets greasy. "Get the Lead Out" brings a heavy coke-boner into America's living rooms. America's drunken, slovenly *id* squeezes itself out of every groove. *Rocks* has got Aerosmith on the cover of *Rolling Stone*. *Rocks* has been all over the radio. *Rocks* is a masterpiece of American consumption, a trash-pop tour de force that defies all analysis and all logic. It is Aerosmith's finest moment.

Government Center

The drums spill out of the speaker before the band picks up the rhythm, a moment of disorientation before the band falls into their groove. Guitar and bass become one, summoning the spirit of Tommy James & the Shondells "I Think We're Alone Now," the spirit of AM radio as the voice of Jonathan Richman burst out of the speaker. His voice, drenched in reverb, rings out like he is singing from the center of the vast, empty plaza at "Government Center."

We got a lotta, lotta hard work today, Richman sings to the Brutalist walls of City Hall. We gotta rock at the Government Center, Richman exclaims in bold defiance of the joyless and oppressive symbol of bureaucracy. Make the secretaries feel better, he sings with a spark of civil disobedience. It is an act of rebellion against the city's self-imposed misery, its capitulation to technocratic efficiency. Richman has found redemption in rock 'n' roll and is ready to share it with the people that need it most.

When the band begins clapping in time with the song, right around the third verse—thwackthwack-thwack, thwack-thwack-thwack—and the organ runs up and through the hand percussion, the entire song ascends to something bigger. We see "the office boys dancing for joy" and we know that music can be a life-saving device, a secular savior beaming out of the speakers. If the secretaries trapped in the bowels of Boston's bureaucracy can feel better, anyone can.

That feeling inside we're going to transmit, Richman belts as the band kicks into double time. It is an ecstatic moment, a verse full of pentecostal movement and snake-handler surety. The band chants, make them feel better, make them feel better, make them feel better as Richman evangelizes. We're going to transmit it to light. (Make them feel better, make them feel better) And with that the bleakness, the darkness, the sadness, are gone.

And then nothing.

The political landscape has changed but only so much. The old protestant ethics and new progressive ideals are still wrestling for the soul of Massachusetts, but the old guard are dying out and a new breed taking the reins. Barney Frank, the former aide to Mayor White, has won a seat in the state house, representing the red light district of the Combat Zone and the South End. Joseph Oteri, the famed Boston Pot Lawyer that fought *Avatar*'s obscenity charges and pot charges for Jon Sinclair, is back in the news, this time attempting to make cocaine legal. There's even talk of overturning the blue laws, the Puritan-era laws that have kept stores closed on Sundays for the last few centuries.

Kevin White is no longer the smiling, glad-eyed hustler he was when campaigning during the Summer of Love. As the 60s turned into the 70s and many of America's second tier cities collapsed in upon themselves, Boston had turned itself around. Ten years of development had brought shining skyscrapers downtown and to the Back Bay, the John Hancock Tower having been problem free for almost a year now. Where so many other cities were burning, Boston was building. The city has changed and so has its mayor.

Rock 'n' Roll with The Modern Lovers hits less than a year after the dueling debuts of the Modern Lovers. Modeled after the buoyant acoustic-driven rock 'n' roll—as opposed to the more contemporary and electric "rock" music—*Rock 'n' Roll*, is bright and joyous. The recordings—Jonathan's first without David Robinson, who had left in mid-'76 for louder pastures—beam with light, bristle with energy. The single "Egyptian Reggae," an instrumental shuffle of oriental delights, hits the charts and brings the band to the Top of the Pops in the U.K. The version of "Roadrunner" from the sessions for *Chartbusters Vol.* 1 is re-released, and making a run at the charts as well. The band's European success filters back to the states, adding to the myth and mystery that surrounds the band. Success still doesn't sit well with Jonathan. He's still wary of the attention that he has worked so hard for, skeptical of the personal sacrifices one has to make to climb the highest rungs of the rock 'n' roll ladder, and so the *Rock 'n' Roll* line-up of the Modern Lovers is retired.

David Robinson is playing with Ric Ocasek and Ben Orr, the former Milkwood bandmates who recently had been playing around Boston as Cap'n Swing. Their new band, The Cars, makes pop songs with an art school detachment, earnest but angular, emotive but not overwrought. Their demo is making the rounds. Their song "Just What I Needed" has been added to the playlists at WBCN and WCOZ. Elektra Records is interested in making a album. For all their art-rock weirdness, The Cars have a dreamy, heartthrob appeal. The pulse of their tunes, the way the synthesizers resonate with the rhythm section gives the entire demo a futuristic sex appeal that belies its bubblegum ambitions. They also look good on video tape.

Jerry Harrison has moved to New York and joined a new band. They've been playing in a basement in the Bowery named CBGB where they've been covering "Pablo Picasso." Talking Heads had tracked Harrison down in Boston, in the hopes that he would join the band. This group had a parallel oddness about them, weird lyrical obsessions like buildings and food, and a deconstructed sense of rhythm that feels like a logical continuation of the style that Harrison had developed with Richman, Brooks, and Robinson. Talking Heads are making something new and the addition of Harrison increases their creative opportunities exponentially.

The J. Geils Band may have missed the mark with their EMI debut, *Monkey Island*. The self-produced record is uneven. The nine-minute title track meanders through heavy reggae and disco-funk jam in a manner that makes for an entertaining live performance but doesn't quite click on vinyl. There is a seriousness to the proceedings that doesn't jive with the band's well-cultivated party anthem reputation. The album misses the Top 40 entirely: neither album nor singles make the big chart. Plans are made for another live album, the band's third, the first recorded in Boston. Monkey Island may have been a misfire but the J. Geils Band isn't going anywhere.

Aerosmith are slightly less popular.

Ernie Brooks: In retrospect, I think Jonathan was right. Maybe we were just too uptight. We were into being this cool rock 'n' roll band, and going "buzz buzz" in the background of this cute little insect song ("Hey Little Insect") didn't fit the image we had of ourselves. Maybe we should have followed him into his vision a little more.[1]

---

[1] Scott Cohen, "Funny How Love Is," *Spin*, June 1986.

Roadrunner (Twice)

Boston ended up doing alright. The 80s saw the city's music scene dominating the nation's burgeoning alternative culture. By the time Jonathan Richman returns with a new Modern Lovers incarnation, the city has become a hub for the smart, art-influenced guitar rock that was dominating college radio and showing up on the *Cutting Edge*, the late-night modern rock program on the newly launched Music Television channel on cable MTV. The J Geils Band, The Cars, and Talking Heads are all prime-time players in the young station's video rotation, and become some of the era's biggest stars. Jonathan Richman hovers around the edges of the music scene, too quirky for the mainstream consumption but beloved by many. By the 90s, Richman would be a fixture on the very edge of popular culture, thanks to cameos in the blockbuster Farrelly Brothers film *There's Something about Mary*. He continues performing to this day, releasing excellent new music every few years.

Aerosmith became a lot more popular.

Kevin White didn't win a fifth term as mayor but the city kept moving forward without him. These days the rent is exorbitant and the neighborhoods are beautiful.

The tech economy has been good to this old college town, the information age a windfall for this ancient city. Neighborhoods that should have been paved over by the Inner Belt are some of the most expensive and sought after places to live. Cambridge is flush with Fortune 500 companies like Facebook and Google. The city is still young, still energetic but the anarchy is gone.

Don Law's grip on the concert industry—it was estimated he controlled almost 80 percent of it at one time—has been split between two out of town corporations. Free concerts on the Cambridge Common are long gone and Harvard Square is closer to a high-end mall than hip neighborhood. The Rat, birthplace of Boston's punk scene, has been a fancy hotel for over fifteen years now. The *Real Paper* shut down in 1982 and *The Phoenix* shuttered in 2013. Mel Lyman might have died in 1979 but nobody outside of the Fort Hill commune's inner circle saw the body. The inner circle still lives around the revolutionary war tower atop Fort Hill. WBCN became a sports talk radio station. There's a greenway where the Central Artery used to bisect the city. It's a safe, beautiful city that has become a model for what cities can offer in the twenty-first century.

The Modern Lovers became a cult classic. The Sex Pistols ensured that "Roadrunner" would become punk rock canon when the British band's sloppy, snotty cover of the track was included on the *Great Rock 'n' Roll Swindle*. "Pablo Picasso" would become a staple in the nascent indie rock scene with covers from David Bowie, Iggy Pop, and TV Personalities, its one chord chug a playground for musicians skilled and unskilled. Rhino Records issued the album on CD with "Government

Center," from the second Kim Fowley sessions, just in time to make sure that The Modern Lovers' legacy was included in alternative rock's self-mythologizing as well. The album has been reissued on vinyl, expanded for digital and streamed all over the world. For a collection of songs that were never meant to be released it has become one of the most beloved and revered in the rock canon.

Bibliography

Bizot, Jean-Francois, *Free Press: Underground & Alternative Publications 1965–1975* (New York: Universe, 2006).

Calvino, Italo, *Invisible Cities* (San Diego: Harvest/HBJ, 1974).

Des Barres, Pamela, *I'm with the Band* (Chicago, IL: Chicago Review Press, 2005).

Heylin, Clinton, ed., *All Yesterdays Parties: The Velvet Underground in Print 1966–1971* (Boston, MA: Da Capo, 2006).

Higgins, George V., *The Friends of Eddie Coyle* (New York: Picador, 1971).

Jacobs, Jane, *The Death and Life of Great American Cities* (New York: Vintage, 1961).

Kaufman, Phil, with Colin White, *Road Mangler Deluxe* (Lafayette, CO: White Boucke Publishing, 2005).

Marcus, Greil, *Mystery Train: Images of America in Rock 'n' Roll Music* (New York, E. P. Dutton & Co. Inc., 1976).

Milliken, Robert, *Lillian Roxon: Mother of Rock* (New York, Thunder's Mouth Press, 2005).

Mitchell, Tim, *There's Something About Jonathan* (London: Peter Owen Publishing, 1999).

Robinson, Richard, et al., *Rock Revolution* (New York: Popular Library, 1976).

Williams, Paul, ed., *The Crawdaddy Book!* (Milwaukee, WI: Hal Leonard, 2002).

Zappa, Frank, *The Real Frank Zappa Book* (New York: Touchstone, 1999).

Discography

Aerosmith, *Aerosmith*, Columbia 1973

Aerosmith, *Get Your Wings*, Columbia 1974

Aerosmith, *Toys in the Attic*, Columbia 1975

Aerosmith, *Rocks*, Columbia 1976

Willie Alexander and the Boom Boom Band, *Willie Alexander and the Boom Boom Band*, MCA Records 1978

The Apple Pie Motherhood Band, *The Apple Pie Motherhood Band*, Atlantic Records 1968

The Apple Pie Motherhood Band, *Apple Pie*, Atlantic Records 1969

The Bagatelle, *11 p.m. Saturday Soul*, ABC Records 1968

John Cale, *Vintage Violence*, Columbia 1970

John Cale and Terry Riley, *Church of Anthrax*, Columbia, 1971

John Cale, *The Academy in Peril*, Reprise Records 1972

John Cale, *Paris 1919*, Reprise Records 1973

John Cale, *Fear*, Island Records 1974

John Cale, *Helen of Troy*, Island Records 1975

John Cale, *Slow Dazzle*, Island Records 1975

The Cars, *The Cars*, Elektra Records 1978

Earth Opera, *Earth Opera*, Elektra Records 1968

Earth Opera, *American Eagle Tragedy*, Elektra Records 1969

Jonathan Edwards, *Jonathan Edwards*, Atco 1971

The GTOs, *Permanent Damage*, Bizarre Records 1969

Jim Kweskin, *Richard D. Herbuck Presents Jim Kweskin's America*

   Co-starring Mel Lyman and the Lyman Family, Reprise Records 1971

The Alan Lorber Orchestra, *The Lotus Palace*, Verve Records 1967

The Modern Lovers, *The Modern Lovers*, Beserkley Records 1976

The Modern Lovers, *Live at the Longbranch Saloon and More*, Munster Records 1998

The Modern Lovers, *Precise Modern Lovers Order (Live in Berkeley and Boston)*, Rounder Records 1994

Orpheus, *Orpheus*, MGM Records 1968

Orpheus, *Ascending*, MGM Records 1968

Orpheus, *Joyful*, MGM Records 1968

Orpheus, *Orpheus*, Bell records 1971

The Real Kids, *The Real Kids*, Red Star Recordings 1977

Lou Reed, *Lou Reed*, RCA Victor 1972

Lou Reed, *Transformer*, RCA Victor 1972

Lou Reed, *Berlin*, RCA Victor 1973

Lou Reed, *Rock 'n' Roll Animal*, RCA Victor 1974

Lou Reed, *Sally Can't Dance*, RCA Victor 1974

Lou Reed, *Metal Machine Music*, RCA Victor 1975

Jonathan Richman and the Modern Lovers, *Jonathan Richman and the Modern Lovers*, Beserkley Records 1976

Jonathan Richman and the Modern Lovers, *Rock 'n' Roll with the Modern Lovers*, Beserkley Records 1977

The Stooges, *The Stooges*, Elektra Records 1969

The Stooges, *Fun House*, Elektra Records 1970

Sugar Creek, *Please Tell a Friend*, Metromedia Records 1969

Ultimate Spinach, *Ultimate Spinach*, MGM Records 1968

Ultimate Spinach, *Behold & See*, MGM Records 1968

Ultimate Spinach, *Ultimate Spinach*, MGM Records 1969

Various Artists, *Beserkley Chartbusters Vol. 1*, Beserkley Records 1975

Various Artists, *Live at the Rat*, Rat Records 1976

The Velvet Underground, *The Velvet Underground & Nico*, Verve Records 1966

The Velvet Underground, *White Light/White Heat*, Verve Records 1968

The Velvet Underground, *The Velvet Underground*, MGM Records 1969

The Velvet Underground, *Loaded*, Cotillion Records 1970

The Velvet Underground, *Live at Max's Kansas City*, Cotillion Records 1972

The Velvet Underground, *Squeeze*, Polydor 1972

The Velvet Underground, *1969: Velvet Underground Live with Lou Reed*, Mercury 1974

The Velvet Underground, *The Bootleg Series Vol. 1 – The Quine Tapes*, Polydor 2001

The Velvet Underground, *The Complete Matrix Tapes*, Polydor 2015

Filmography

Danny Says, dir. Brendan Toller, 2016
Zabriskie Point, dir. Michelangelo Antonioni, 1970
Chelsea Girls, dir. Andy Warhol, 1967
The Thomas Crown Affair, dir. Norman Jewison, 1968
The Friends of Eddie Coyle, dir. Peter Yates, 1973
Fuzz, dir. Richard A. Colla, 1972
Jonathan Richman: Take Me to the Plaza DVD, 2003

Websites

Discogs.org
Jojochords.net